Growing Up True

Growing Up True

Lessons from a Western Boyhood

Craig S. Barnes

FULCRUM PUBLISHING
Golden, Colorado

Library of Congress Cataloging-in-Publication Data

Barnes, Craig S.
  Growing up true : lessons from a Western boyhood / Craig S. Barnes.
    p. cm.
  ISBN 1-55591-350-4
  1. Barnes, Craig S.—Childhood and youth. 2. Arapahoe County (Colo.)—Biography. I. Title.
  CT275.B4472 A3 2001
  978.8'8203'092—dc21

                              2001002332

Printed in the United States of America
0 9 8 7 6 5 4 3 2 1

Editorial: Marlene Blessing, Lori D. Kranz, Daniel Forrest-Bank
Design: Paulette Livers
Cover photograph: The author as a young boy, taken by the author's
    mother, Thedia Barnes

Fulcrum Publishing
16100 Table Mountain Parkway, Suite 300
Golden, Colorado 80403
(800) 992-2908 • (303) 277-1623
www.fulcrum-books.com

For Will, Lisa, Tom, and Molly

Acknowledgments

In the beginning was the word and just a little before that was Mrs. Fredrickson, who brought confidence and language to a lonely fourth grader afraid of his own gifts. In eleventh grade, Mrs. O'Connor read Amy Lowell and Emily Dickinson, as if words and truth were locked together with pure beauty. Morgan Farley and Amy Rennert offered strong encouragement when the writing was beginning and the obstacles were great. My wife, Mikaela, fanned the flames of the writer's life in our first love letters and has never stopped, over more than forty years, encouraging the writer's craft. Without her encouragement, this book and most of the other good things in my life would have never happened.

Contents

Preface

Frank and Erik thought that a person could become a man if he was to fix fence, pull wire, skin logs, wear out the gloves. My mother thought that same person would develop moral character if he would carry water to her maple saplings. *Not the close ones by the house,* she said, *but the far ones, over by Savage's wheat.* My father said a small person should learn to plan ahead, think a problem through, be lighthearted, cheerful, ready to help whenever needed. It would also be good to do the algebra homework, and geography, too, and it would be good to clean the barn, and it would be good not to be so sullen on just any old gray February afternoon.

Which was fine. But a man needs the thin edge of the sword every now and then. My father said, *Well, forget the sword, this is not Horatio Hornblower country. Swing a sword around here and you might stick a chicken.* So there was the real world and there was my world. I was ready to cast away on a frigate for the Indies, but the only water around was the Highline Canal, which was dry all winter and in summer washed up at City Park Lake in downtown Denver, definitely not the Indies. I wanted to twirl from a lanyard in a typhoon, maybe save a king. Nobody in Arapahoe County knew what a lanyard was, but it was right near there with great waves and winds and frigates and some kings and I liked the combination. *Well,* said the father—who substituted for king in most situations— *the rains come and the winds blow and the universe does not stand still for small boys who swagger. Cheer up and pull the weeds in the asparagus.*

This is to say that in cottonwood country there was no way for an ordinary boy to become a man without serious mental bending. Frank said to skip the Woolworth's candy: "leave it lie," he said, and "save your egg money for college." Erik said that if a person was to clean his chicken coop and keep the boards tight on the hog pen and keep the irrigation ditch cleaned, all on a regular basis, this would be a person who pretty much had the makings. Work and Erik were like slop and hogs. He thought it would be honorable to die of exhaustion. "Get it done now . . . won't have to do it tomorrow," he said.

It didn't make any difference, as far as I could tell. Tomorrow, there was always plenty of wire still to pull. Erik just naturally liked to sweat and huff and pull and yank on things. My father was a victim of the same attitude. He said, "Try holding off acting brave and proud, swaggering your hips when you are only carrying water buckets to the pig. Brave and proud is not needed to slop the hog."

Out where we lived, the most important things were wheat and calves and a long walk under the cottonwoods to school. In spring the wheat greens up slow and in fall the leaves brown down slow. Summer races by too fast to get a grip before Fair is over and Curtis School begins its annual program of small-boy-mind numbing. I never saw a stagecoach hold up or a real shoot-out or a revolution to overthrow the Mexican government. We never discovered gold after 1858 and there had not been a calf rustling even in the memory of Mrs. Fredrickson, who had been teaching school longer than I had been alive. If Fredrickson did not know, it was not known. There was therefore almost nothing ever to be brave and proud about except sneaking up on ground squirrels or winning a horse race or surviving the great Big Bend suicide.

Still somehow I eked brave and proud from nothing. This is the story of how I did it. Other people have the fortune to grow up deprived. They can complain and snicker and dishonor the rich. We grew up lucky. Enough money for weekly hamburgers. Snickering generally disapproved of. Every advantage except one and this was permanent. I was the youngest. My two older brothers sat through and passed Mrs. Post's math class with flying colors, as if they were born to know certain stuff. They could also turn a lathe and they could ride Smoky the gray mare like Apaches on the wind. I could ride that mare until I hit the sharp turn at the Big Bend and fell off. I could not pound a ten-penny spike worth a darn. It was too big and I was too small. Things like that upset a man. Over the years it was pretty much the same. No matter how much smarter I got, my brothers stayed ahead, like lead cranes in a V going south and I flapping along behind.

My father said I could learn how "cheerfulness comes from work," sort of like freedom from slavery. So this book is about how cheerful comes when a person is corral-gate high, until he gets to about the age where he starts pressing his Levi's to impress certain people of the other type who stand by the fence and watch when he goes past. This is cottonwood and wheat country, the 1940s, the Great War just over. The time we got was borrowed from a world that was always fighting. My parents were trying to make me reasonably honest, honorable, hardworking, and humble. I was just a little too attracted by what is wicked and famous. It took awhile to get everybody stretching the same wire.

I.

The First Leaving

THE RUSSIANS CALLED IT the Great Patriotic War, a name far more hallowed than simply World War II, as if wars could be numbered without meaning, or as if we might say here's one, there's another one; this one's six, that one's seven. The Russians still speak about that conflict as if the history of the world turned upon that one great event. And they were right. At least they were right for me. It changed my history, too.

The Russians sent off 20 million, and I sent off only one. But I remember how that one was sent, and how it was the end of one time and the beginning of another.

I remember how the five of us were crammed into the '41 black Chevy, how we drove into the mountains for one last camping trip. How on Monday he would be gone. How this one weekend, this winter campout, was supposed to hold all the memory, hold all the love, be a symbol, be a metaphor, make the leaving be only physical, but not real, not in the heart, not where it mattered.

He drove, of course. He always drove in those years. And I remember her in the front seat beside, the three of us wedged in back. *One last chance to have fun,* she said, *before he goes.* She wouldn't say, "before he goes to war." That would let in some recognition, the unspeakable, that war and death go together. So she just said, "before he goes," and we sat grimly, the three of us under twelve, me coming on to seven, knowing that wherever he was going it would be uncommonly long this time, and it would be awful. There was snow in the forest. The black road turned and weaved through the hills. The wind was cold. God had not picked good weather for our last weekend.

We twisted and turned until finally my father stopped in the middle of some desolate cold woods and said, as he always did, "This will do."

He led the way into the forest beneath barren trees and tromped down snow to make a place for a fire. Then we scattered like refugees through the woods searching for dry wood. I remember how frosted leaves crunched under the thin crust; I can still hear their crushing sound, can still feel my cold toes. I don't know what month it was, but it was winter on our faces, winter as we hunted for dry firewood, winter in our hearts, winter at the beginning of the Great Patriotic War.

My woolen mittens soon were sopping wet, and then my fingers hurt. In no time I stood by the fire site stomping my feet, holding my arms, whimpering. Snowy branches, snowy leaves. No place to sit down. Snow on my steaming shoes, inside my gloves, in my eyes; blubber rolling down from my nose. For once my mother seemed helpless; *wait,* she said, *the fire will be warm soon.* But there was no hope in her eyes. This fire would not warm her fingers. This fire would not cure her cold. She would not show it, of course. We were all having our last weekend, and she wanted his memory to be sweet.

Somehow we slept the night there in the snow. We rolled thin sleeping bags as close together as we could, and each time anyone moved, which was all the time, I awoke shivering. In the morning there was no cereal, just leftover steak from the night before. Cold steak in the snow tasted too salty, too dry, too much like the last supper. Then we drove silently home. On Monday morning she put the three of us boys on a school bus and said that when we came back he would be gone.

I came home that afternoon under a dusky sky to a quiet house. There were no lights on. I found her sitting alone in the living room. Darkness slid down leafless branches to hover at the window where she was staring. I crawled into her lap. I did not know what she knew. I did not know what war meant. I did not know where Germany was. I only knew he was gone. *Our gentle, good man,* she said, *would be gone a long time.* A very long time.

I do not remember that ever before I had seen her so sad. I began to cry. She held me. I went on for a long time, whimpering softly. She did not say anything and I did not say anything but she kept me close.

The sun went down. My brothers came in. I sat quietly in her arms. For us the war had begun.

2.

The War Effort at 23rd and Holly

AFTER MY FATHER'S LEAVING, my mother thought London had become the world capital. She listened to war news before, during, and after dinner. Frank and Erik talked about landings, air raids, and Germans. "You can contribute to the war effort by not making such a difficult face," she said at dinner. Maybe she did not realize that I was seriously facing down a mess of beets. The war effort was part of everything. It seemed to require cleaning up the yard and forgetting absolutely about chocolate. I did not think the Japanese would make me eat beets and secretly thought that rice might be better, so I was slow to clean up the yard.

We were outside the city of Shreveport on that last weekend when father left and it was out near the Louisiana bayous that I watched the darkness fall while sitting in my mother's arms. But Louisiana was not home. The Army had taken us there. It took us before that to Tucson, and before that to Iowa, and before that to Virginia, and before that I don't know. *We will go wherever he goes,* my mother had said, *as long as they let us.* And so we were in Shreveport when he shipped out, but she looked around and said that that was not where she wanted to wait. She wanted to be near the mountains, where she could see the sky, and watch the storms coming. So she packed us into the black Chevy and drove to Denver. We moved into the attic of one of her old friends. The lady's husband was in the Pacific and she was a stickler for table manners, which meant she was like us. Then one day my mother found a red brick bungalow at the end of the streetcar line at 23rd and Holly. There were four rooms, high elms, and a narrow strip of grass. *We can wait here,* she said, and rented the place immediately.

Mornings, afternoons, late at night, she waited by the radio. By this time, the Allies were crouched in England ready to pounce. She liked to listen to Ed Murrow: "This . . . is London. . . ." Murrow's voice was like a preacher's on the first day of school. "This . . ." he said, "this is London. . . ." He was like somebody announcing a measles epidemic, only once in a while you could hear the bombs falling. At first, when we were done with that, my mother allowed me to listen to Jack Armstrong the All-American Boy or Yukon King. Later, when times were better and she could look around and see the evil effects of idle time on her third son, she clamped down. She did not approve of boys lollygagging around the radio when they could be out in the fresh, open air, cleaning the yard. But in the beginning, she was concentrating like everyone else on the weather over the English Channel.

One day, riding my bike home from school, to my great surprise I was suddenly flying through the air and then skidding along the concrete gutter on my elbows. I had hit a car. It did not hit me. I hit it. Before that time I had thought I was more or less like everyone else. But that day I learned I was a serious space cadet. Just before I hit the car I was looking up, dreaming a cowboy song, all alone in my own world. Suddenly this black vehicle was in my way, so I hit her. A very flustered lady stopped and rolled me up into her backseat. She put my broken bike in her trunk and asked angrily, "Where do you live?" I had definitely ruined her day.

I wanted to cry, but looking at the woman to consider the prospects for sympathy, I decided against it. She did not look happy and, anyway, a person in the war effort was not supposed to talk to strangers. Someone might be listening to pick up little secrets. Especially when a person was hurting, that was when he might tell a secret to some spy. Like, *My father is in England. Ohh,* she would say, *and what is his unit? Oh,* I would say, *he's in the Engineers,* and that would be like putting butter in Hitler's hands. We all knew that. So I just sat in her backseat and did not cry. The lady maybe thought I was a spy, too, and did not say a word until we got to my house. "This will take care of you," she said, trying to get her distance. But then, just in case I was a normal kid, she said, "You should be more careful."

"Yes," I said, "I know," not giving her any secrets, either, and dragged my bike to the front porch and laid it down to die forever.

Just for the record, we eventually lost a lot of tanks and battleships in the war; we also lost one bicycle.

Maroon, with nice white trim on the fenders and a fine black seat. Aunt Betsy, my mother's sister who was visiting from California, heard me moaning over this loss on the front porch and came out to look me over. She looked at the bike, the wheel shaped like a right-angle corner, and then looked at me, seeing the bumps on my head. I was a little bloody. She said, "I think we should find a doctor, don't you?"

I just hung my head.

She said, "I just don't know where there is one. Your mother will be home pretty soon. She'll know." Betsy was older than I, but she was more pretty than old. She said she thought a doctor would tell me if my head was broken.

I didn't want the details. I had already lost a bike; if my head was broken I was not going to be able to clean up the yard or any other useful thing that would help me become a man. I had done about the dumbest thing a kid could do, running right into a car.

My mother came home. She said that a doctor would be unnecessary. She was not pleased. I said I missed my dad. She said she thought I had been daydreaming again and she missed him too. There was a war on, and it was no time for daydreaming. I got my hands and elbows bandaged and the blood cleaned off my head. I did not get any extra sympathy. I had to walk to school after that. Erik said that if the bump on my head was hard enough, it might be an improvement. Frank said when there is a war on, people get hurt, that's all.

We went hiking on weekends high up in the mountains, near timberline. It was a Saturday routine. I went straggle-mumble along the trail to Lake Isabel or Brainard

Lake. There was a lot of going up: up along creeks, up over boulder fields, up over rocky, wind-cold passes. My mother thought that going up was good for the kind of moral weakness that led small boys to drive their bicycles into cars. She said these walks made us all stronger. Unfortunately, hiking over the passes at ten thousand feet, I usually felt nauseated. The thin air made me even more spacey than normal. I wanted to lie down a lot. I thought everyone else got altitude sickness, too, so I never mentioned how I felt, except to hang back and look down at the ground. I was sure that my brothers had each overcome their weakness and it was only a matter of time before I would overcome mine.

The week before Christmas 1944, I discovered a shiny, wooden tommy gun in my mother's closet. I knew it was for me. The good news was, I wanted a tommy gun really badly and this was a good one. The bad news was, I couldn't seem to enjoy it once I found it. I felt scared and unhappy. I sneaked into my room and lay on my bed, expecting to be struck dead.

A few days later, on Christmas Eve, lying half asleep, I pretended not to see my mother come to fill the bedside stockings. I was hoping that there was not a real Santa Claus who kept a list of who was good and who was the kind of person who would go spying in closets. Then, in the dark of Christmas Eve, I listened to the crumpling of little packages sliding into the wool sock that was pinned to the window above my head. My mother left the room. I opened one eye slowly and felt the sock. It was full and near overflowing! I was probably the only person in the world so happy to find out that there was no Santa and no list.

Half the world was fighting; the other half was waiting. Every Sunday night we were summoned to the dining-room table to write a letter to my father. We called him by his first name. I said, "Dear Don: How are you? I am fine." That was that. Two sentences. It would have been good to say something about the tommy gun or the bicycle wreck, but those were tricky subjects. So I stuck with being cheerful and made a little decision not to let the truth spoil the occasion.

The radio told us about the Allied invasion of Normandy. We held our breath. We saw stars going up on gold or purple banners in windows in the neighborhood. People were getting shot up and the stars told us who they were, or at least where they lived. They told us who was just wounded and who was killed in action. I tried not to stare at them. When Don's letters came, my mother read to us the things that didn't give away any military secrets, like the colors of flowers or sunsets on windy nights in France. Then when she got to a certain part of the letter, she wouldn't read outloud anymore. Her eyes got wet and she sat like a little girl, hushed and sad. "This is for me," she said, waving us off. Erik grimaced. "This is the mushy part," he said. He tucked his chin into his chest and he and Frank left the room. I followed them and went out to throw tennis balls against the front steps to "get rid of excess energy," which is what she called it. Of course, we never knew if there was too much mush or not enough.

One afternoon my mother folded up a letter and said abruptly, "Boys, I am going to go to church." She had never done that before. "Clean up your room," she said over her shoulder.

Two or three hours later, she came home red-eyed and pale. I had never seen her cry and she was not crying, really, but she looked a washed-out wreck. The three of us watched her come into the house and hung back. We went to the bedroom to play where she would not have to look at us or hear us. We did not fight or throw pillows or any normal thing. "Shh," said Erik.

That was as close as I ever saw her come to breaking down. At dinner Frank said, "This war has gone on for nearly at least too long."

She nodded. She said we should be glad he was all right, physically. That's all she said. I suppose there were other ways he might not be all right, but I did not know what those would be and she was not talking to little kids about it. She missed him, I think, even more than I did the day I ran my bike into a car.

It was coming on toward the end of August 1944. Saturdays, we went up to the mountains, where I practiced getting sick without complaining, and on weekday mornings I began loitering at the end of the trolley line, which terminated right across the street from our house. Every fifteen minutes a wooden car rolled up the tracks. The driver, in a black motorman's cap, hopped out and pulled the wires to the back of the trolley, and that was all he had to do to reverse directions. Then he took his money box and tickets, hopped back in at the other end, and was pointed back downtown. There was a paper boy selling the *Rocky Mountain News*. "Read all about it! Allies Advance! Only a nickel! Yes sir! They are into Paris!" Or, "Yes sir, they're moving this morning! Only a nickel!" It seemed like the nickel was pretty important to him, so I learned about money and later on I started learning about the war. The boy said that the Allied armies were crossing the Rhine, and then the Russians were moving in on Berlin. The News carried cartoons of *Willie and Joe,* who always seemed to be sitting in the mud with bullets buzzing past their helmets. I hoped that Don was okay physically, wherever in the mud he was.

Since he was in the mud and I was on high ground I thought I should do my part. I volunteered to help the paper boy and pretty soon I got my first grown-up, real-life, paid job, racing around among the men who were hurrying to catch the trolley. I earned a flat 35 cents a month, which the newsboy thought was too much. He did not think a little kid could be worth that. But my mother said I was, so I held out for the full 35 cents, which meant I had to sell at least seven extra papers a month just to make it up to him. I surely did that. He got his money's worth, just like my mother said. This was my biggest finance deal of the duration and my mother said that it was not war profiteering.

We did these things and the war ended. Maybe we caused it to end, maybe not. This was my part. I sold newspapers and kept the people happy at the corner of 23rd and Holly, in Denver, Colorado, in the USA. Other people had other corners, and some may even have had bigger jobs. That's all right. I did the best I could, and since it was my first job, I did it better than any other job I ever had.

One day there were sirens and horns honking, and our family climbed into the black Chevy to go down to the center of Denver to mill around and shout and sing and listen to clanging church bells because there was victory in Europe. "This is something the boys should see," said my mother to her sister, Betsy, who still didn't have a husband and didn't have much to do out there on the coast without one, so she was visiting again. So we all went down and saw the big celebration. It didn't matter that it took forever in all that traffic and that there was no place to park and that thousands of people crowded the streets. It didn't matter at all. Everyone was happy. Holding hands in a string of five, Aunt Betsy, my mother, and three boys, we washed back and forth like seaweed in waves of people who were shouting and singing. Paper was flying, church bells ringing, trolley cars clanging, horns honking, men and women hugging and kissing, and everyone acting like they knew everyone else, like brothers and sisters. Betsy did not get kissed because she was surrounded by three kids and her sister. Otherwise I think she would have, because she was very pretty. We five sloshed around in this sea of delirious people until my mother thought we would never forget it. Then we went home, having learned what it was like to win a war. I thought all the men had gone over to Europe to fight, but that day there were quite a few still left in Denver.

"Now go clean up your room," she said the next day, "and get ready. He'll be coming home."

Then there was a kind of numb time. One day while we were waiting for the troop ships to get to New York, I asked her what it was going to be like with him at home. "Will we still go to the mountains if I don't get sick so much on Saturdays?"

"What's this, 'get sick on Saturdays'?"

"I always get sick when we go hiking," I said. "It's all right. I'm used to it."

"Oh," she said, as if for the first time since my father shipped out she could relax. "I didn't know." She opened her arms and drew me to her. "You did your part," she said, "you really did."

Then she added: "It will be okay . . . ." Her eyes sparkled. "He will be like the father of fathers."

I looked at her. "What does that mean?"

"He was a good man," she said, "and the war won't change that. I really don't think it could change that."

But everything about our lives was going to be different.

3.

The Return

IT WAS AUGUST 1945 and the house under the elms was tense. There had been telegrams from Paris and New York and from along his route home. He would come by train to Fort Logan, near Denver. At ten on a Saturday morning he would come out, meet us at the gate to the old fort, and walk away from the war. He had been to England, France, and Germany and that was probably most of the world. He had conquered Europe, but he would be standing alone at the gate at Fort Logan, waiting for his wife to drive up and take him home. "Hello, soldier. Hop in," she would say, and then we would drive back and get on with life. The world should have been shouting or playing a grand march, and there should have been crowds and ceremonies, cannons and whistles. There should have been something that made it easier not to talk, because what in the world were we going to talk about?

Hitler was done for, and Europe was wasted, Ed Murrow told us from London. Millions had died in Russia. Berlin had fallen. One of the great battles in the history of the world was winding down. Now the man who knew all about it was going to be standing at the gate at Fort Logan with a duffel bag and a uniform. He would be about five-feet-eight and black-haired and dark-eyed. The last time I had seen him had been 18 months earlier, the night we slept out in the snow in the mountains of Arkansas when I was crying and whimpering. I figured I had to show that I was beyond whimpering now.

"I don't want to have an accident," she said, carefully driving out of town. "Not at a time like this." In the backseat, we nodded. Who was going to say what to whom? Even a kid knows somebody is going to kiss somebody, and what was that going to be like, after all those dry, dry months?

Erik did not hit me or shove me, and this was a signal that he was not feeling normal. Frank sat frowning. I sat motionless. I was last in command and I would stay last, but this did mean one more boss at the top. "I don't want to have an accident," she said, again, as if we had not heard her before. We stared straight ahead. She drove so slow I could have run to Fort Logan faster.

We turned the corner and could see the gate in the distance. It was a half mile away. After a while we could make out two figures waiting in the sun, looking toward us as we came creeping down the road. Gradually the figures became soldiers, and one was standing straight as a post, his hat pulled forward, no slouch. At the wheel, my mother mumbled recognition. "There he is." The '41 Chevy was going to break down for sure, she was riding the clutch so bad. I do not believe there was another human being within a hundred miles. The gate was not busy. The Fort was empty. The plains of Colorado were empty. We rolled up slow so caterpillars and grasshoppers and other innocent beings would have plenty of time to get off the road and no one would suffer just because of our happiness. The other soldier was not ours, but the first thing my mother did when she got out of the car was to smile at the other man and say, "How are you?! Welcome home!" She had to be polite, first, of course. Or, just maybe, the other man was the easy part. Then she looked at my father.

From about ten feet apart, they moved toward one another. Halfway there she threw open her arms and he moved quietly into them. They kissed fiercely and then held on hugging one another. He let her go at last and one at a time he hugged the rest of us. I was the last one to hug. He had to keep reaching down lower and lower. I was too scared to laugh or cry or say even one word. I don't know how his duffel got into the trunk. We had a father back. The idea had become a person. I hugged the person and waited to hear about Hitler and the invasion and the boat ride home. In the front seat they talked about his train ride across the country, about whether either of them had slept at all, ever, whether he had clean clothes with him, whether now he had anything he had to do for the Army anymore. They talked like water bugs on the surface of a lake. We were all trying so hard to be nice it was like inside a refrigerator in there.

I was not sure whether soldiers gave presents so I did not ask. This was not like before the war when he used to go on maneuvers for two or three weeks. This was way more serious. When we unloaded the car back at the little brick house at 23rd and Holly, I stood around and stared at him. He stood around and stared at our house. "Well, this is fine," he said, and I saw that he was polite, too.

He dug into his bags. I thought to myself, maybe guns, or helmets, or bullets, or grenades, or German medals, or maybe his medals. Maybe stories of fighting and maybe he was a hero, maybe something about the Bronze Star he had got or the Croix de Guerre he had got from the French. He pulled out some waxed paper and inside were sticky, greasy ball bearings. He held them up. "These are very smooth," he said.

We three boys were sitting on the floor at his feet. He handed each of us a little waxed paper package that contained concentric circles of hard steel wrapped around little balls, packed in heavy grease. We nodded solemnly. The grease smell was peculiar, not like anything I had ever smelled in Denver. "They are from a factory in the Ruhr Valley," he said, "and they are very nearly perfection. The Germans were very fine craftsmen."

We waited to hear more, maybe of some excitement or flames or fire. To get the ball bearings out of the factory, it had to be in ruins. But he seemed unwilling to tell any story of war or the walls coming in on the factory or any such thing. "These are very highly machined," he said quietly.

Germany was in ruins, rubble from the Elbe to the Rhine. The dust of it was still in his boots, the horror in the crow's-feet by his eyes. "We can't lose sight . . ." he said, slowly turning the ball bearings in his hands and then drifting off. Maybe it had been a long time since he had been with people with whom he could speak softly.

My mother waited standing, unable to sit down; she looked as if she were wondering if she should bring some tea or say something. Her known world was changing the way it does when you come over a high mountain pass and suddenly see valleys and high peaks and river canyons all in one gasping instant. And he? What was he thinking? The man was sitting for the first time in years as the head of a family in a chair he did not know in a house he had not seen, with three small, but definitely larger, boys sitting in a circle on the floor at his feet. There was no right thing to do, no polite thing.

Frank said, "Now that the war is over, do you still have to wear your uniform?"

He was in Army dress, his silver lieutenant colonel's oak cluster on his shoulders and red and blue ribbon bars above his left pocket on his chest. His face was bronze, his eyes glistened, and he looked at her: "Thedia, I guess we'd better go shopping." She beamed. No one had said "Thedia" like that for a long time.

Still no one moved; no one knew what to do next.

He looked down at us on the floor. We were still trying to figure out what to do with our packets of greasy ball bearings. He said finally, softly: "You're wondering what these are. Why I brought them home." We nodded.

He said, "You have to look for beauty, even here, because you forget sometimes. Fine is fine," he said softly, "even on the other side."

There was something so simple about that that I thought I was going to melt. I turned my head to look back over my shoulder at my mother waiting near the kitchen. Our eyes met. I thought maybe she was remembering our conversation about what kind of man he would be. A tiny smile crept around the corners of her mouth. *See?* her eyes said. *See? What did I tell you?* She drew in a long, deep sigh, and I thought maybe she was melting too.

There were not, that afternoon, guns or bullets or helmets or stories of fighting. There was no talk about Hitler, and for us that chapter was over. He just brought home one small thing that showed that even on the other side there had been people for whom quality was important. He never said a word about revenge or forgiveness or what it was like to be in a winning army in the greatest conflict in history. He just brought us ball bearings that were the smoothest and finest in the world, which had not been made by us, and told us to look for beauty where we could.

4.

Crossing over from the Last Frontier

THEY CAME OUT OF THE MISTS, as best as I could tell, the two of them. My mother was born in New York, or maybe it was my father who was from New York and she was from Pittsburgh. They did not put much store by either place, and both cities were pretty surely, as far as I could tell, east of the Platte River, maybe even farther than Kansas, but not all the way to Europe where the war had been. Places east of Kansas were history, like old photos, probably important during the Roman Empire, which was about at the beginning of time. Pittsburgh and New York were the same in one important respect: they were not in Colorado.

Later on, when the conversation turned to who we *really* were, my mother liked to say that somewhere back on my father's side was a Lord Mayor of London and on her side were shipbuilders from Maine, the Sewalls. These included Samuel Sewall, who burned witches at Salem and then later repented. Samuel saved his own soul by saying he was sorry. "A little late for the ladies who burned," said my father, wrinkling his nose.

Still, we considered the Sewalls and the Lord Mayor worthy enough ancestors. Somewhere in the basement we had a piece of dark paper on which was a charcoal rubbing. It was supposed to have been taken from a gravestone that was on the wall of a seventeenth-century cathedral somewhere in England. The rubbing said that the deceased lady, one Anne Sewæll, in addition to being extremely reverent and devoted to God, was incidentally a "worthy stirrer up of others." My mother liked that. She liked to needle Republicans and quote Anne Sewæll. *Politics comes to us naturally,* she said, *we are from a long line of stirrer uppers.*

We never did find out the exact name of the Lord Mayor or when he was, or why. But he and Anne Sewæll were our connection to flags and trumpets, even kings, and I liked kings especially. We could claim London by way of New York, Pittsburgh, even Maine. I liked the idea of trumpets and red and gold carriages and great men who were kind, or kind men who became great.

There was also South Bend, Indiana, where my great-grandfather got shot. He was innocent, they said. He was standing on the boardwalk on a dusty July afternoon, minding his own business, when a couple of desperadoes started a shoot-out. My great-grandfather was in the middle. His wife and my grandmother, still a girl, were living in the country outside South Bend. One day men on horses came galloping out to the house to tell the news. *Ma'am, your husband has been shot. No, it was not his fault, but yes, he is dead.* The little girl—my grandmother—had watched the men ride up all lathered and upset, and she looked up at her mother, who was taking in the news, absorbing it, holding on to her composure, trying not to crumble and be a weak woman in front of those wild riders. The sudden widow just stood still, stunned, as if a tidal wave had hit the rocks. The rocks did not crumble. She did not cry. And that was the story in our family. Things happen, even bad things, but crying is not any solution.

It was unfair, of course, losing a husband like that, and senseless and, except for the fact that anger is a waste of time, there would have been rage. *Rage wastes energy and blurs a person's reason,* as my father later said, *and that's not very productive.* So the story was that unfair things happen, that's all. The widow Montgomery and my grandmother were left alone and they had to make do. They moved on, in the manner of the frontier, in the direction of the Oregon Trail to the West, where a woman with neither a husband nor credentials could still find work teaching school. So in addition to the Lord Mayor and the witch burner, there was the ancestor who slowly bled to death on the boardwalk of South Bend, and there was Oregon. And most of all there was someplace called the frontier where a person could start over fresh without being judged just for being poor.

Of all the places he could later claim, the frontier was the one that my father spoke about most dearly. The frontier had freed us, he said, from something called social class and from failure. I did not know what "social class" was, but I could tell from his tone that it was something they had a lot more of than they needed in the East, and the Lord Mayor was probably right in the middle of it, and that it was a kind of baggage that held some people down but not us, not now, not out here in our West. I was attracted to kings, and the Lord Mayor seemed like a good deal to me, but my father seemed to think we owed more to hard work and a new start than to all those flags and trumpets.

My grandmother eventually grew up and went back east and married a dashing young man on the move, one Barton Barnes. He was more dashing than on the move, really. As an organizer and camp director for the YMCA, he could barely put soup in the kettle. The family, who after a while included my father, wandered around the Midwest from rooming house to rooming house in Kansas City; Independence, Missouri; and Manhattan, Kansas. During the First War, times were so bad that they ate "water soup" for lunch, which was nothing more than a mixture of hot water, butter, salt, and pepper. Finally Barton decided to take them back to Merlin, Oregon, to sell real estate. The family crammed into a small cottage that was without heat or running water. It was cold and uncomfortable, but it was the frontier, and it was natural to be miserable when starting a new life. Barton quickly failed again and once more departed town. My grandmother and my father were then left alone in the peach orchards ten miles from anything like a town. Barton had gone looking for work back east. No one knew where that was. He didn't say. They didn't hear from him for a long time and when they did, he did not sound like he was anxious to hurry home.

My grandmother had to make money any way she could. She began teaching school out of their cottage, there in the summer-green fields of central Oregon. "Mom," as my father's mother was called then, invited into her school a family of three girls who lived on a nearby hill. The father of that family, Frank Schellenberg, ran a sawmill over by the Rogue River, a ways beyond the forested turn in the valley. The mother was the fifth daughter of a New England minister and was an artist. She was writing an opera and was interested in politics, music, and drama. Her grandfather had run for vice president of the United States with William Jennings Bryan in 1896. So she was a somebody. She liked drama about as much as a person could like drama, and deep subjects and tragic endings—which is what you get used to if you have anything to do with William Jennings Bryan. Her father had been a Swedenborgian minister and his relatives before him all the way back to revolutionary times had been ministers, so she claimed that God was part of the family. She did not question that the Eternal was part of the Schellenberg woodwork. Swedenborgian men were intellectual, informed, critical, and philosophical. Mrs. Schellenberg was mystical and dramatic and definitely in touch, as in In Touch. She was connected to the men and women who would be in direct contact, so it seemed to us, with God. Swedenborgians were very rare in Oregon or anywhere else in the world for that matter, which made Mrs. Schellenberg feel as if she had a mission. She had a lot of missions, when you think about her opera and her religion and her girls and politics. She did not have as much time for the sawmill.

Donald Barnes, my father, by then was in his late teens. There were yellow buttercups and white Queen Anne's lace and green grass everywhere over the hills. Apple and peach blossoms were abundant and spectacular. The first young girl to come to Mom Barnes's school was Thedia Schellenberg. Thedia was named after a certain Captain Thedia who had sailed the seas in the nineteenth century; it was a hallowed, special family name. But that was natural: Schellenbergs liked things special.

Don Barnes was interested in things being efficient and thought girls were by nature inefficient. He was more attracted to diagramming sentences and Latin conjugations or someone who might teach him ancient Greek. He would do anything to keep from ending up as a YMCA camp director. He was about to become high school valedictorian in Grants Pass.

Thedia had been home-schooled by her mother, learning all about Constantine's Arch in Rome. She may have known more about Constantine's Arch than anybody west of the Mississippi. She knew where, when, why, how wide, and how high. She knew the friezes and the generals on horseback. She did not know anything else about Rome. But her mother had a picture of the Arch and so she knew the Arch. "That's almost the same as knowing ancient Greek," she said to Don shyly.

He liked a straight line and liked to think about the consequences before he drew one. Thedia couldn't be bothered with thinking about the consequences; she liked sparkly, wiggly streams or flowing green hills, everything that was not straight. He could not prove

God, so he kept this question at bay, a sort of permanent silence. She did not care about proving God. She knew. He was part of the woodwork.

"Well, they'll keep each other awake," Mrs. Schellenberg would later say.

When Thedia arrived in the Barneses' peach orchard, she said she simply needed a new teacher and had heard that Mrs. Barnes had sufficient books to be able to go beyond the Arch. She had long brown hair down to her waist and an easy, throaty laugh. She loved to tease and it didn't hurt that Donald had fine, curly black hair and deep brown eyes, nor that he had a soft voice for singing cowboy songs and a gentle, winning shyness of his own.

At this time, Thedia's father did not know as much about sawmilling as a person ought to know. It was harder to make a profit than it was to tell good stories, and Mrs. Schellenberg was better at the stories than at keeping books. So all in all, the Schellenbergs were on thin ice in Oregon. Then the sawmill burned down in the middle of the night and the ice broke.

Both families were down to thin gruel. Thedia came down the hill to the Barneses' peach orchard and into a family with a shot-dead grandfather, a mostly absent father, and neither she nor they had any money. Taking into account her own two sisters and perpetually ecstatic mother, there were a lot of women around. But there was only one stable young man.

The backgrounds were dramatically different: the one side, through Grandmother Schellenberg, was into passion because life was all an opera. The other side was into denying passion because it was the sort of danger that might take a man away and, in the case of Barton Barnes, they might never see him again. What the young couple had together was this: she needed to find a real, safe professional, more skilled than her dad, and he needed desperately to be one, so as not to be like his dad either.

How they worked it out to get from the peach orchard to the altar is a dark secret. He, the budding engineer, was opposed to getting carried away about anything and, of course, she favored it just a little bit. But since they differed in this they never talked about it.

By the time I came around, love was reduced to a few slogans: a man ought to know better than think that love is a full-time thing, or that you can pay the bills on love, or that you can love a girl without checking out her mother, or that love is easy, or that you can ever change a man by loving him, or that the man will ever love the woman as much as the woman loves the man. This was a territory where caution was advised. It could be magic, it could be poison; for safety's sake, consider it poison.

So we were from the frontier by way of Constantine's Arch, courtesy of the Lord Mayor of London and the Sewalls of Maine; we were from an unsettled land, where we all get a second chance, no social status, and are the better for the lack of it, unless "it" was running on a losing ticket for vice president. That episode was perfect: high status with a failed result. *We should be classy without class,* he said shyly. *Christian without excess,* she said, as if feeling out the words of moderation. Or, *Christian in your heart and the form will not*

matter, and she gave up her attachment to four genera-
tions of Swedenborgian ministers. *Professional,* he said,
but without pride. Yes, she said, *and if you are blessed
with good fortune then quick to the aid of the laboring
man and widows and orphans. That would be good,* he
agreed. *We could have some fun,* she said. *We could try,*
he said, not exactly disagreeing. *The West is like that,*
they said together softly, *and that's where we are from.*

5.

The Blizzard of '46

WHEN THE HOMECOMING WAS OVER, differences showed up in my parents' conversations about pure, raw enthusiasm and about religion, about his caution and her tendency to leap forward.

He was a checkbook balancer, but she would say with an easy smile, "Oh, I'm sure there will be enough." He was a planner. She was a "well, yes, but-let's-stay-flexible" person. She would say, "I think we could get to California in about twenty-four hours, if we drove straight through," and he would say, "Well, maybe thirty." Across the pauses in these sentences, she could still see the horrors of the war in the crow's-feet by his eyes. They had to get on, past something he would not, or could not, talk about. Only now the easy romance of the Oregon hills was no longer a quick start. Their differences were even more pronounced than before, deepened by the months of separation. I was just a little kid. But I could feel it. They needed the new start that the frontier brings.

She made it sound like a mother's concern. She said that the air is healthier in the country and that small boys who might have a tendency toward juvenile delinquency could be kept busy cleaning harness or pulling weeds, or fixing fence, or chinking a barn, or tethering lambs on the grass for mowing.

Erik, now at thirteen, wanted to be a cowboy so bad he was threatening to steal a mare from the milkman. Frank, at fourteen, was a man with an unnatural interest in school, especially equations. He was sort of neutral about the move to the country, since gravity probably works just as well out of Denver as in it, but objectively speaking, one could probably make a go of life anywhere, considering, that is, all the angles and the expense of things.

With this analysis we got into the '41 Chevy and drove around south of Denver until we finally found a couple of acres next to a sumptuous brown irrigation canal lined by great shuddering green cottonwoods. My mother stood by the banks of the canal and gloried in the overhead sunlight dazzling in the leaves and glittering on the brown water or shining in the golden wheat stalks of the fields. Then she said, "Oh, boys, see the clouds tumbling along the prairie horizon!" She laughed and dropped her voice and was embarrassed because this was too much exuberance.

Still, later, when the house was built, in an evening storm when winds blew and cottonwood leaves shivered fiery sunset-orange, I would watch her standing for minutes at her kitchen window, just looking. *This feels like home,* she said when I came upon her.

It does seem like our natural habitat, my father agreed at dinner. He was an engineer and an officer and a father, but there was some kind of poet living in him. When the season came, he directed our attention to the grass that points yellow stalks up through thin December snow and he showed us where tiny mice tracks curled in under the gray sage, reminding a walker that he's got company. He was friends with the nontalking world; my mother was awed by its beauty. That was enough to start with; the two of them could make a new home and not talk about the war or whom he had met there.

So they built a house out in Arapahoe County, with some land under cottonwoods and a place to breathe. The whole package, land and house, cost $11,500, which concerned everybody but my mother, who just said, "Don't worry, somehow we will still be able to send Frank to college." And so I did not worry. Really, I wasn't worried in the first place. College was not much on my mind. It was okay for Frank because he had a slide-rule head, but I immediately took to exploring the buckbrush and squirrel trails or lying flat on my back in the hot dry grass of summer, watching magpies drifting on the wind. I had my mother in me.

In this house, for the first time in my life I had a bed of my own. I was glad to get away from Erik. In the double bed at 23rd and Holly, he was a wiggler and a rib jabber. Now we also had a dining room where a gilt-framed old lady hung on in a grand portrait on the wall. She was a certified nineteenth-century battle-ax. My mother was embarrassed because it was her ancestor, so she said, "I think she has a stomach-ache, don't you?"

Still, since the woman was named Thedia and came from our nineteenth-century family, we had to keep her up there, glaring down on dinner. The lady had an old-fashioned white lace cap on her head.

"What's that for?" I asked.

"To remind us that she was female," said my father.

Outside, there were two and one-half acres of grass, or weeds, depending upon your perspective, which usually depended upon your age. Everywhere I looked I saw grass. Everywhere my parents looked they saw weeds. My mother attached me to weeds like hot is to soup. In her mind we were meant for each other. She wanted me to do it quickly; my father wanted me to do it carefully. In this case, I was like neither one of them. I didn't want to do it at all.

There was no furnace. Times were hard, the war was only just gone, and my father said all the furnace parts were rusting in tanks outside the fields of Stalingrad or in battleships at the bottom of the North Sea. The contractor, a certain Mr. Hobbs, promised a furnace in about six months. "But Mr. Hobbs is very hard on his wife," said my mother, so she thought it would be more like a year. She was the only one who knew why those two things were related.

"I don't know that it has much to do with Mrs. Hobbs," said my father.

"Well, sometimes Mr. Hobbs says one thing and does another," said my mother, who secretly thought Nell Hobbs deserved better. So we expected we would get a new furnace either when the tank makers switched to furnaces or when Hobbs started treating his wife better, depending upon your point of view. Anyway, it was August, so I didn't worry. *They would clean up Stalingrad by winter,* I thought.

"I can watch clouds gather from Pikes Peak in the South all the way along the Rockies to Longs Peak in the North," my mother told her friends in the city when she talked on the phone. "I can see storms along a hundred miles!" She was pointing to shining gray and white peaks that spread the whole length of her front window, framed by giant cottonwoods at the corners, and in the middle of the picture, 14,000-foot-high Mount Evans. She pointed with her hands even when she was on the phone, because that is the way she was.

Then one day in November, the wind began. Dried leaves swirled down from cottonwoods along the irrigation canal and bumped around the little white house, which stuck out alone and without cover on the prairie. Dry grass stalks, brittle and yellow, bent away from the hills, pointing east. In the West, great Mount Evans disappeared. Clouds, smoky and brown, came down to tree level and it began to snow.

It was one of those storms where white patterns shear in wind-driven sheets off the roof or dive in solid curtains past the windows then leap up and swirl with a clatter against the siding or suddenly drift still in front of the big window holding out a single motionless flake for a small boy to stare at and then miraculously the whole white world lifts upwards and over the chimney. In an hour there was already an inch laid down. In four hours there were six inches and drifts were rising to a foot. It was the kind of storm a person can't stop watching; it held me to the window, hour after hour, looking, turning away, then back again to see what grass or bush had gone under. "You boys had better get more wood," said my mother, and the three of us went out into the storm.

We had to bring in a lot of firewood because Mr. Hobbs still was not treating Nell right and so we still had no furnace. The wind was stinging, flakes were flying in great swirls and building up in two-foot drifts. It was okay, though, really. I knew that not just anybody can wade through blizzards and high drifts and carry in life-saving firewood. I did not know a single person back at 23rd and Holly who could have done that. As it turned out, Frank and Erik carried in boards of leftover lumber from the house construction, but I carried in medical supplies just off the dogsled from Nome, Alaska, and, unknown to anyone else, saved the whole town.

Nobody seemed to notice. "It seems tight enough," said my father with a twinkle when we stomped back inside, because he was still thinking about his new house and for him things tight meant good work, craftsmanship. "It seems tight" was high praise for the carpenters who built our house, now being tested by 30- to 50-mile-per-hour winds. "See here," he smiled, pointing to the base of the casement with pride, "the windows are solid." Then he sent us out again where it was not tight, to find a place where the blowing wind had stripped the construction lumber bare of snow.

During the fall months before the storm, we had had to spend afternoons hammering nails backward out of scrap wood so as not to waste the nails or the wood, I'm not sure which. We had coffee cans full of bent nails.

"Useful some day," said my father. "Yeah," said Erik, who liked hammers, "come on, Craig, get a hammer." So that's what we had done that fall for Erik's recreation and my moral improvement.

"Why don't we burn the wood and collect the nails from the ashes?" I suggested hopefully, thinking as usual about ways to lessen the effort.

"Nails would be ruined," said Erik, who never said more than he had to. "Come on, let's get it done." He had an unnatural love for work. It was probably because he was in charge. I was permanently not in charge. It was my life's condition.

It was November 1946. It snowed and blowed. There was still as much snow going up as there was coming down. The house was cold in all the corners, in the kitchen, in the bedrooms, dining room, everywhere except directly in front of the fire. "A furnace would be good," said my mother wistfully, after about the first four days. We dug in the drifts and listened for KMYR to tell us if it was going to let up or continue or get worse or bury us forever. Day after day, we carried armloads of scrap lumber into the living room, knocked the snow off, and threw it onto the fire. Sometimes my shivering mother would have mercy and fix us tea. "Have some tea, boys," she said cheerily. "That's marvelous! We will be warm all night, don't you think, Don?" He was our analysis man.

"Might be," Don said.

"Might be" was polite for "probably not." It was not his fault, though, and before bed we went out again into the storm. We crashed the snowy lumber down into the wood basket by the fire and waited to hear his answer. Would it get us through the whole night?

The snow was coming up to the windows. Before we turned in, she brought "tea," which was hot water, milk, and sugar and not tea really because we were not yet of an age to be allowed the highs of caffeine. Sometimes we had hot chocolate with marshmallows, which was also caffeine, of course. But hot chocolate did not bring to mind the dissolute society world of the East Coast or of the social classes of London or of the theater or the arts, all of which were suspect on the Arapahoe County prairies. Chocolate was okay for boys; coffee was not. There was nothing the matter with chocolate morally. Only, of course, it was more expensive, which in those years was next closest thing to a moral flaw. So we didn't have chocolate very often and real tea never. Coffee was not even considered. No liquor. No cigarettes. No bad thing. If a person was not careful he could end up getting carried away and drifting off to someplace irresponsible, as Grandfather Barton Barnes did. Stay away from coffee, you bet. I could see the sense of that.

The radio said that schools would be closed. This was not bad news, but I was careful not to say anything out loud except "Well, that will be nice," because a smart man does not gloat or tempt fate. As soon as I would get cocky and say something like "Whoopee!" the storm would leave. I was not born yesterday; I was smart enough to know that. This strategy worked. The wind continued to pound the windows with heavy flakes. We could not see across the valley to where cars ought to be inching up University toward Curtis School and the eastern county. Either the snow was falling too thick to see that far, or the roads were too drifted over for any traffic to pass, or both. There were no lights, only darkness outside, but inside there was a circle of firelight. "Monopoly would be good, don't you think, Donald?" she asked. "I think so," he would say when nothing more useful could be found, after which the rest of us kneeled around the Monopoly board on the floor by the fire.

Sometimes he would put aside his engineering and settle into the big chair with the *Saturday Evening Post*. It was a signal he could be coaxed into reading out loud about the lives and fortunes of Babe and Little Joe or Tugboat Annie. Amazing children got into desperate scrapes in the practically wild West or out on the heaving whitecapped sea. But somehow they always worked their way to safety in about three or four installments. Sometimes when he read "Amazing Children," without missing a beat, he would sneak in the words "like Frank, Erik, and Craig" and go on reading as if it were in the magazine. When he did that, I would look at my mother questioningly, and she would let that tiny smile creep around her mouth the same way she did when she was standing in the living room that day he came home from the war, as if she were saying again, "See, what did I tell you?"

When the *Post* story was over, if it was not really complete, we looked for something called a "Postlude." I have never heard of anything like that before or since. But sometimes the best horse died or the old, kind aunt drifted off and never came back, and this was a bad way to end. So a Postlude was supposed to ease the pain. Yes, the stallion died, but his colt grew up to be a champion. Or yes, Indian Sam got lost, but years later they heard he showed up down in Tucson and was still saving kids from rattlesnakes. The best serials, to my thinking, were always the ones with six or eight installments and a Postlude. Then we knew we would get a reading every week all the way to Christmas. The *Post* came on Thursdays and we almost always had Don persuaded to read out loud by Saturday or Sunday night. Three serials was barely worth it. Four was average. Eight was a secure future.

First we had to dig him out of those engineering magazines. When we saw the thin-print book fold and the right hand move toward the *Saturday Evening Post,* we squirreled onto the couch or knelt by the fire. No one said anything, lest he change his mind. He read honey-sweet and soft when the sun was out, and hard when the snow was blowing and Babe and Little Joe were in trouble. On the couch my mother knitted. She could make sweaters with deer or elk or snowflakes, necks rimmed in white zigzags. She knitted so many sweaters when he read that, over the years, we each got more than one. A good story could get all the way from the waist to the pattern. I rolled yarn or sometimes just listened with my head in her lap. This was not a scary time. Even when the stories were supposed to be pretty tense, I never got really worried. The father of fathers was reading. He was usually more worried than I was. When Babe and Little Joe got through everything, usually in the last column of the last page of the last installment, a lot of times he had to get his handkerchief out. He blew his nose and grinned and wiped his eyes. The way it worked, they almost always got through a blizzard to find the injured horse or saved a lost cow and were invited into a dark warm cave by a secret Indian friend. I could have told him and saved his handkerchief, I guess. I was sure. He read like wind brushing through cottonwood leaves. I knew that life was good and the ending would be fair or honest or kind; it had to be or he would not read it to us.

Sometimes if we had already read the *Post*, she said, "Shakespeare would be good, don't you think, Donald?" and then we all took parts in *Hamlet* and read aloud about poor Yorick's skull while outside there was no moon to be seen and snowflakes pelted the glass. Then, at last, she thought all this was enough. "Hot chocolate with a marshmallow will send you off," she said. After which we three boys sneaked away to the covers and crawled deep down to get maximum warm. I, secretly blissful in the knowledge of a tomorrow and tomorrow and tomorrow without school, listened to the wind scraping twigs back and forth along the house and fell into dreamless, holy sleep.

6.

Prairie Rain

AFTER THE SNOW MELTED in spring, it rained.

"It's good for the crops," said my mother, but I knew she had mixed feelings. The road out front was not paved and sometimes there was hubcap-deep mud all the way round the house. Our trail to school through the wheat field was oozy, and on rainy days the way to the corral was squishy slop. In cottonwood country rain meant mud in the kitchen, living room, bedrooms, everywhere. But water was good for the wheat, so my mother had to talk positively when she was at the feed store or talking to strangers. Even at dinner she took the high road about wheat and corn, but I knew that, really, rain meant mud. Rain was good the way Mrs. Fredrickson said it was good to learn myths of ancient Greece or the way my father talked about volunteering to help someone in need. Good at some real high level, but bad on the back porch. This is probably where a farm child learns that everything has two sides. A man has to accept mud because someday the hay will come.

Along the irrigation canal was a two-wheel track for the ditch rider, and when snow melted or rain came, it turned to pretty near pure squish. City people sometimes would try it anyway. They liked to follow along the canal past a stand of cottonwoods and then around a great corner where there were picturesque high cliffs and a prairie-dog town. We called that place "the Big Bend." The ditch turned slow and easy and the dirt road widened so that a family could pull off the track and have a picnic in the tall timothy grass by the water. Sometimes cars would inch down there at night and stay parked for a while. During the rainy season, Denver people would come out any time of day, get nosed in down there, and sink into the mud. There they would sit. This was good for my sense of who was who. Sometimes we would slosh out along the road and push one of their cars out, modestly but knowingly.

"If they had asked us," I said, "we would have told them not to go down there."

"Especially when the water is standing in puddles and the snow is melting slow," said Erik. "A person should know that slow snowmelt makes more mud than rain." Erik was good at observing anything down on the ground near to grass or crops; he was born with dirt and sticks and stones all naturally in his brain. "They ought to know that."

"Maybe," I said, "in the city they separate water so well that they never saw it mix with dirt."

"Maybe," he said, "but there's no point, really, trying to explain city people." We were well on the way to forgetting we had ever lived in a city.

One night, up there along the wheel tracks under the cottonwoods, lightning was flashing and storm clouds were raining in buckets onto the Colorado clay, and from the house we could see glints of light on a sedan that was stuck up to the hubcaps. There was a black hulk in a black night about two hundred yards from the house.

"Best help," said Erik.

We got our coats on and sloshed out into the night. On the way, every now and then, the lightning would hit out on the prairie and make the car glisten. We slopped up and knocked on the window. "Need any help?"

The window didn't open. It was quiet and we could see nothing in there. So we yelled again, "Need any help?"

Slowly, inch by inch, the window came down. There was Jack, from school. Maybe three grades older than I. He was fast on the football field. I knew him because we were wrestling one night on the bleachers during a football game and I pulled him down and he hit his side real hard on the corner of a wooden bench and nearly died. He didn't die right then or even look too bad, but we all stopped roughhousing and he started looking pale and later his family rushed him to the hospital with a ruptured spleen. Then they nearly lost him. We stopped roughhousing in the bleachers forever after that. Now, on this rainy night, I knew who he was and that he was one fast football player. The window came down and Jack didn't have his shirt on and his skin gleamed bright in the flashes of lightning. Hovering beside him, kind of scared, birdlike, was the prettiest little blonde girl I ever saw. She was maybe checking out the injured spleen.

Jack said no, he would be all right.

I had a hankering right then to get better acquainted with Jack and his friend who was checking his spleen, but Erik said, "Let 'em stay stuck," and we turned for home.

One other drizzly day the whole family was out working in the back corral and we heard a screech out on the front road. Then a car spun around, scattered gravel, and headed back down the road toward town. My father left us for a little while, quietly, without saying much of anything and went up by the cottonwoods where the car had taken off. He came back and talked quietly to my mother, who whispered to her sister Betsy, who was visiting again because she still hadn't got a husband, and then they all whispered together.

My father got the car keys and left without any kind of explanation, but we knew it was about the car that had raced away down the road. My mother just said that he would be gone for a while.

The next day we learned that when he had gone up there under the cottonwoods, he had found a young woman lying in the dripping grass. The lady said she had been thrown from the screeching car. So my father bundled her up in a dry blanket and took her somewhere safe in Denver. It was a sleazy incident, but sopping-wet women in the drizzling rain is not the sort of thing that our kind of people talk about. At least not to children. I guess the lady was hurt and I guess my father helped, but we never talked about it.

One of the things that everybody was sure about was the whole problem of getting carried away. I figured both the woman who was lying in the grass by the road and my friend Jack had got carried away by the same thing, whatever it was. Once or twice I tried to listen to the *Hit Parade* on the radio, but that did not last long. *Too much of that romance business can get your mind off your work,* said my father. *You'd be better off rechecking your spelling.*

The original person to get carried away must have been my grandfather. We talked about him only once, on an afternoon by the big chair in the living room, for about ten minutes. Don made some rare comment and I realized I hardly knew a thing about my grandfather, a man I had never met. I said, "What happened to him?"

Don stopped what he was doing. He straightened up and stood motionless for a little while. I could see his face cloud up. He said: "Well, Pop just drifted away. He went away and left us. After a while we never heard from him again. It had to do with finding someone else, I guess." He said these sentences slowly, as if he were pulling his body through heavy sand.

"Finding someone else?"

"Yes, I suppose that was it."

"Never heard from him at all?"

"No, he just left. Some men make that decision," he said. "You can't tell, really, what were the reasons for it." I saw that his eyes were getting wet. "We don't know for sure what happened to him. Maybe it could have been something else."

"Was he nice?"

"He was nice, yes. He liked to come inside on a rainy day in Merlin and we would all read together sometimes. He liked a good story."

"Do you miss him?"

He turned and reached for me, wrapping me in his arms. "Well, now, I've got you three," he said. "That makes up for quite a lot."

He seemed not to want to go on. I hugged him, squeezing so tight that maybe it hurt his neck. We stayed that way awhile. The subject changed itself. Like turning a page. The sad book about his father was ended.

We never talked about his pop again. So there was that once for about ten minutes.

We were quiet about difficult things in our family; we did not talk about men being rude to women or leaving them or about Jack in the car or the woman by the road. They were all related to the dark world where people get carried away. It was better not to mention things you did not want to encourage or have happen again. So instead my father talked generally about "the early days." He said in the early days in Oregon when they had been a family, when the wind blew and the rain came, they had all come indoors and they were together then. That was what rain did. It brought you indoors. It didn't mean stuck cars or lightning shearing off cottonwood branches or the wheat knocked down. For him it meant the time before the lonely time before my grandfather went away. Rain reminded him of the early days and the whisper of a warm fire and a late book with tea, everybody there.

I changed my mind about rain. You've got to have rain and some place to read and talk to keep women and children from ending up out in the cold or on their own. That's how I figured it. If it had rained more, my grandfather might have been with us, never gotten carried away, and my father would not have been so sad. After that I understood why my mother said, "It's good, you know. It's good for the crops. It's good for all of us." It was the "all of us" she was interested in, probably even more than the crops.

In the first months after the war, there had been letters to my father in a woman's fine flowery hand. They were postmarked from France and made my mother go gray. She knew about the world where people get carried away. And she knew what it was to have a home. They were the two ends of the world for her. Whenever it rained, she took advantage of it and we played games around the fire or had milk tea, or she asked my father to read a story. After I heard about my grandfather, I knew why she did it. Rain can keep a family together.

7.

The Major Leagues
of Arapahoe County

IT MUST HAVE BEEN LATE APRIL or early May 1947 when I taught Arnie Coughlin how to swim. Snow was melting in the mountains but the peaks were still white. It was also still cold on the prairies of Arapahoe County because that time of year there is some sun, some rain, some gray drizzle, and some little bit of summer leaking through. This was not one of those days when the summer was leaking through. It was about three in the afternoon, and we were ambling home after school, walking in the narrow dirt rows between greening wheat shoots. Darryl and Arnie were there because we all lived across the wheat from school and usually walked home the same way. That day we came to the top of a little rise from where you could see all the way to snowy Pikes Peak in the South and snowy Longs Peak in the North, maybe a hundred miles both ways. To the East you could see all the way to Brazie's horse barn before the plains shaded off into Kansas. Closer down below was a row of cottonwoods, thick alongside the Highline Canal. We were shuffling along swinging black lunch boxes, probably talking about skunks and calving season or the general ignorance of people who live in cities. When we came to the top of the rise, suddenly we could see down into the big ditch. This day, for the first time in many months, the canal was running full broad and brown, flowing quietly between two rows of giant cottonwoods. The appearance of water meant winter was officially over and irrigation season was beginning at last. It was the countdown to school's end. Within weeks it would be Field Day, the end of classes, haying season, County Fair, and night after night through the lazy days of summer, sleeping out in the tall grass alongside the ditch under the stars.

"Ditch's in!" yelled Darryl and we took off running, swinging our lunch buckets around our heads, stumbling to the water's edge. We slid to a dusty halt in dry soil on top of the brown cliffs above the Big Bend. About fifteen feet below, slow-moving dark water carried all the refuse of winter, everything that had been piling up in the miles and miles of sandy ditch through the long months since the last run of August.

The moving current looked as cold as slush and I said quickly, to sort of get my defenses up, "My mother won't let me swim in this."

"That's silly," said Arnie immediately.

Arnie specialized in making little kids feel littler. "You ought to. Mothers don't know much about swimming in the Highline Canal." I looked at him skeptically. My mother was not so bad.

"Mothers used to be girls," he explained. He chortled wickedly. Arnie was always good at explaining the rules to referees whenever we played football or to younger grades whenever they almost won some playground game he was in. He seemed to know a little more about how rules that we thought were rules were not rules, really. He was in direct contact with some upper world governed by muscle and brawn in which rules were not rules, the same as most little kids thought. "On the first day," he said, "when the ditch has to be washed out, there is going to be dead sheep. Sure. But to say that a person don't have no right to swim in the Highline Canal just because once't there was dead sheep is just dumb." Arnie was looking off into the distance toward Kansas as if consulting with the source of knowledge for people with big muscles. His own arms were like steel pipes. He milked every morning and night and hayed all summer and was good with his hands. "Beats me about dumb women," he said. "This first day when the ditch runs there are always logs and boards and pop cans and such, but they don't never hurt nobody." He looked at me. "Except maybe city kids."

I was only about a year out of the city. Arnie had touched on a serious character flaw and I knew it. I looked down at the brown water and saw fluffy yellow creamy foam drifting along in big clumps, but I did not see any dead sheep. Arnie said, "There are not very many dead anythings, really, practically at all."

I stared at him, wondering how he could be sure. "What a person has to do," he said, "is get into the water before he gets home from school before his mother has a chance to make up the rules. The best thing to do is swim now and when you get home say you didn't know you weren't supposed to."

Arnie and I were in the same class. He was bigger and older but he did not think much of school and every now and then he didn't mind repeating a grade. He knew more than I about cows and horses and haying and most everything to do with an irrigation ditch. It made him nervous, on the other hand, that in mythology class I could keep track of how to plant dragon's teeth in order to raise an army and in geography I could spell Boise quick as a beesting. He didn't seem impressed that I was always raising my hand. One time he told Darryl that Craig was okay in school but not much good for real things, things you could use in an actual useful life.

Now he was pushing and I knew that something was not quite right, but I could not tell what. I hesitated, looking down at the quiet, cold water.

He spit out, "Race you across!"

I started pulling off my clothes. Coat, shirt, shoes, and pants fell onto the dirt. I had some serious point to make about my character because even though I once lived in a city, it had been at least a year ago and it was time for the stain to be erased. If he wanted to race, he was going to get it. I could race. I could swim. Scrawny is not so good for stacking hay, but scrawny is no problem for swimming. I threw underwear and socks on top of the clothing pile at my feet. Arnie seemed to be moving real slow. I jumped over the side of the cliff, bare heels gouging into the sheer dirt, and slid vertically to within a couple of feet above the water, then opened my arms and lifted off into the air. The diving wasn't so bad, in fact that was my best moment, but the coming down was not good. I hit the water with my chest and there was more crash than glide. It was water that had very recently been snow, just off the mountains. My chest went instantly tight and all the breath went out. I popped my head up and sucked for air, gasping and flailing the brown water with desperate winter-white arms. I was vaguely aware that strange things were floating past. Thick clumps of yellow foam gathered in my hair and glommed on to my face. Paddling around the floating things seemed better than going under them because it was black down there, and colder, and unknown. I sputtered and flailed twenty feet through drifting sticks and bottles and emerged on the bank on the other side. I scrambled up into the tall grass and stickers and tumbleweed, shaking furiously. Creamy foam and bubbles slid down my shivering back and pink legs. This had not been a good idea. *I should quit this*, I thought. *Yes, definitely, I think I will quit this. That's enough.*

But now there was a serious problem. My clothes were on top of the cliff on the other side. Not good. Not smart. Where was Arnie?

I danced up and down but my feet were being punctured by tumbleweed stickers and cottonwood knobs hidden in the prairie grass. I couldn't just dance there all day. I sure couldn't stay over there with the April wind freezing little globs of ice on my arms and legs. No sign of Arnie anywhere. I would win if I lived. I calculated I had about ten seconds to die, to freeze stark naked next to an old gray cottonwood trunk that spread out over me. "There's the Big Bend," they would say someday. "There's all those pretty cottonwoods, and there's our little Naked-Boy Tree."

I wheeled around, tiptoed through the grass gingerly, and plunged again into the dark water. Better to die trying than to freeze into a little naked-boy tree. My arms and legs motored brown water into white as I sped across toward the cliff on the other side. When my fingers hit mud I popped out like a frozen cork and scrambled up the cliff, clawing filthy dirty up the bank. I pulled up to the flat on the edge of the wheat field, dripping icicles and mud, gasping. Darryl and Arnie stood motionless.

"I don't know, I just don't feel like swimming this year," Arnie said.

"It would be better," Darryl said, "not to catch cold this near to baseball season." I knew then that I could swim better than either of them. I knew I had won, but it was not clear that this would help my reputation. They might still think me a city kid. In fact, there was something about the victory that made that more likely.

I shivered into my clothes and stomped. I had won a great swimming race but still didn't feel so good. I wanted to be proud, since I had found out that neither one of them had the gumption to swim and I had just done it. But both Arnie and Darryl were looking a little glum, too.

Being chicken is almost as bad as being a winner, I guess. So we looked around and didn't say much and I shook and shivered, pulling on my clothes, sitting on the ground trying to get the mud off my feet before I put my socks on. After a while Darryl picked up a stick and hit a rock out over the brown water.

"Want to hit some homers?" he asked, trying to change the subject. "Bet I can hit past that big old cottonwood!"

"Okay," Arnie said, "no problemo!"

"Over the ditch is a double. Over the wheel tracks is a triple. Into the alfalfa outaway ova there is a homa!" Sometimes Darryl could not say his Rs so he said "ova" instead of "over." He and Arnie started talking about baseball season but I was all through with heroics for one day. We shuffled on home and I had the problem of having had a big adventure but not being able to tell anyone about it because I wasn't supposed to do what I did. I felt miserable. "Don't let anybody fool you," Erik said sometimes, usually when he was sitting on my back holding me pinned to the ground. "Boyhood is not as good as being older and smarter." He was small for his age, so he probably knew. That advice had not sunk in at the time because it was hard to concentrate when he was sitting on my back. But I remembered it after the great swim race and wished the speed with which I became older would hurry up.

I did not give up on baseball altogether. My mother regularly listened to the Brooklyn Dodgers on the radio, mostly when she was ironing and needed some excitement bigger than flattening collars. There was no earthly reason for her listening to the Dodgers or for being loyal to Brooklyn, which was definitely a city in the East, but that is what there was on the radio and there was not a single major league team west of the Platte River. So it was the Dodgers or the Giants, and the Giants were from New York, which is hard to root for in most circumstances. "Our Dodgers," as she put it, included Ralph Branca, a pitcher, Gil Hodges at first, and Jackie Robinson at second. My mother said it was very exciting that Jackie was a Negro, which we did not have any of at Curtis School but which my father said would be okay if we did. At least the Dodgers had one.

Darryl and I got to be as good as Jackie Robinson by hitting rocks out on the gravel road in front of the house. There were mailboxes down the road to mark a single, a feeder ditch with bunchgrass for a double, a giant cottonwood for a triple, and over the far fence was a homer.

"And here comes Gillll Hodges!" Darryl said one June day, stepping out onto the road by the old tin mailbox, our usual location for home plate. "He comes to the plate, fans, with the bases loaded." Darryl had a good announcer's voice. "Pee Wee Reese is at third, Jackie Robinson is at second and, and . . . NO! NO! It's Gil Hodges at first and COMING TO THE PLATE is that Colorado hometown boy wonder, DARRRRYL BARTLEME!"

At this sudden attention from Darryl the announcer, Darryl the batter is going to get serious. He has a kind of shy smile on his face and reaches down to the road for a right-sized rock. "Fans, look at the lumber he is carrying!" Darryl the announcer is enthusiastic. "Bartleme is at the plate now. No. He steps back . . ." Darryl the batter puts the rock into his shirt pocket and reaches down again, his smile slight, his confidence great. Babe Ruth, I know, is modest in the face of brilliance; so is Darryl. Bartleme the batter slowly scoops road dust into his hands while Bartleme the announcer sighs in wonder. In the Big Leagues any decent hitter will take time to dust his bat. The old wood is mostly gouges, chips, and cracks at the hitting end. That end is now poked into the dust at Darryl's feet, the other end cradled across his thigh. Darryl the batter scoops up a fistful of dust and smoothes the handle, careful not to run his fingers down toward the cracks and splinters at the hitting end. Darryl the batter does it thoroughly, taking time to drive Darryl the announcer and all the listening thousands mad with impatience.

A few feet behind him, I lift my eyes to the top of the tallest cottonwood and raise my chin into the air. I croon:

Falstaff beer is the right beer, yessiree,
Falstaff beer is premium quality . . .
Choicest product of the brewer's arrrt,
Always call for Faaalstaff.

Darryl the announcer is ready. "Fans, Bartleme's back at the plate now, Reese on third; Robinson is taking a big lead at second, Hodges holding on first. Fans, this looks good. The Colorado Wonder is at the plate, bases loaded. He is looking eager today, folks, he really is." Darryl the announcer suddenly stops and looks at me: "They say Bartleme has 25-inch arms from feeding and watering livestock when he was a boy. That's what they say, ain't it, Red?"

"Yes." I don't miss a beat. "That's right, Dizzy, Bartleme is a horse-feeding man, he surely is. And they say he can lift a 200-pound grain sack easy as a horse's hind end!" Darryl the batter is only partly pleased with this assessment but he is confident. He softly and carefully throws a small rock two feet into the air. There is a light wind blowing from left center, beyond the tallest cottonwood. There is a mighty swing.

"Stee—rike one! He swung and he missed!" Darryl the announcer is amazed.

Darryl the batter is a little embarrassed. He has swung and made the air tremble; he has swung so that farmers in Kansas are not safe, but the rock has fallen, plunk, and puffed up a little dirt at his feet. Darryl the announcer moves to save the day. "Don't worry, fans, I have never seen the Colorado Wonder look so hungry . . ."

He pauses. "Here's the windup. Here's the pitch . . ."

"Craig!"

It is my mother somewhere off in the distance. She is way out of the stadium, nowhere near Ebbetts Field. It is surprising that we can hear her over the noise of the roaring crowd. "CRAIG!"

Darryl the announcer looks at me, annoyed. Darryl the hitter is appalled, waiting for quiet, like a preacher waiting to preach. "Just a minute!" I yell up over the bleachers so it will carry all the way from Ebbetts Field to the little white house in the wheat fields of eastern Colorado. "Just a minute!"

"Stee—rike two!" Darryl the batter misses again. Darryl the announcer falls silent. Darryl the batter is in trouble. No word is spoken from the playing field. Tension settles over the rocky road out on the prairie of Colorado where the cottonwoods have no end and Darryl Bartleme is meeting a life challenge.

I try to help out again:

Falstaff beer is the right beer, yessiree, ...

I fill the airwaves while he searches for a rock of just the right size.

"Craaaig! Come in now, this minute!"

It is hard to become a star in Arapahoe County. I knew that already and was going to learn it a few more times before I was through. Just as the Colorado Wonder was about to hit a king-size home run beyond the most distant cottonwood, farthest ever in the recollection of western man, I, Red, the singer, was called in to carry water to my mother's saplings. The apple and the ash and the maple trees would die without my buckets of water. *Now,* she said. *Right now.* "If you don't do it when I remind you, you will forget," she always said.

I don't know how many major leaguers there would have been from Arapahoe County if we had not had to feed and water every morning and night. It is a shame how work gets in the way of greatness. Darryl's career ended with two strikes, a dead rock, and a splintered bat and I never even got my turn.

8.

One Mighty Fine Fence

THE SPRING AFTER THE HOUSE WAS UP and the blizzard was behind us, my mother had started buying six-inch seedling trees. She stuck a whole bunch of scrawny bits of trees out in the middle of the prairie grass with a little stake beside each one so that small boys could find them with buckets of water. That year we carried a lot of buckets. Then my mother started digging a hole in the ground to plant asparagus roots. The hole was about fifty feet long, which was going to be a lot of asparagus, but she believed that boys who are digging asparagus do not become juvenile delinquents.

Don built a combination radio–record player into the corner of the living room and fixed a lathe in the basement to carve table legs. Frank got a slide rule and began to assay things too complicated to do on paper. Erik set his sights on becoming a cowboy. He walked like one, talked like one, surveyed the far horizon for storms, and was good with a rope. He could drop a loop over a bush at ten feet, unless he or it was moving.

To practice roping while moving he needed a horse. To get a horse he needed a corral. To get a corral he needed a fence. To stretch wire he needed a little brother.

A fence is pretty much a fence, really. Holes in the ground, posts, wire, staples, a wire stretcher, and any man can do it. That is how it seemed to me, anyway. But Erik enlisted my father and that is not how it seemed to him. For starters, once the hole was dug and the post was in, Don liked to tamp it down with an eight-foot, twenty-pound steel bar. Ten, twenty times, he threw the bar at the base of the post, hammering down the loose dirt. He was trying to make a post stand like a steel tower. "More dirt, Craig," and he went on lancing the earth with the bar until at last he was exhausted. "Wiggle it," he said. I tried leaning on the post. It did not wiggle. Then he leaned his 175 pounds against the cedar and heaved with all his might. Still no wiggle.

"It might not wiggle now but the rain will loosen it," he said, and hefted the twenty-pound bar again. I watched his arm muscles bulge as he thrust the weight into the unyielding earth, again and again. "Will have to do," he muttered finally, panting, laying the bar down and moving slowly on to the location for the next posthole.

Some men sink posts as if they were planting seed: near to the top of the furrow is good enough, or close to the line will hold a horse the same as dead on the line. But some men don't consider a fence a monument. For my father, anything he did with his hands was a sort of announcement to the world: We are careful here.

He jumped on his spade and chiseled another hole two feet down into the hard Arapahoe County clay. This time on the way down he hit rock. Probing left about three inches, he found clean soil and chiseled again, slashing around the stone with his spade. Together we got down on our knees and dug out scoopfuls of loose dirt with our hands. "Atta boy," he said. "Now hold the post." He went up the fence line to sight over the line of posts. "No, not quite." He came back through the weeds to where I held the post. "That rock has got us. Rascal! The top of the post sets up a good three inches east. Pull it out." I wondered why three inches could make any difference; it would have been hard to imagine how a cow or horse could care.

He dragged the twenty-pound bar from the last hole to the new one, lifted it two feet above the hole and thrust downward with all his might, hurling the bar at the rock in the clay which had made his post three inches off-line. *Whang!* The sound of the crash rang out across the fields. A quarter mile away in Bartleme's horse pasture animals raised their heads in question. *Whang!* Rocks in the hole shattered under the steel blow. *Whang! Whang!* Like a frenzied man killing snakes in a pit, he seized the bar and threw it down, seized it and threw it down. *Whang! Whang! Whang! Whang!*

When sweat was pouring from his back and shoulders and he was heaving for air, he laid the bar in the prairie grass and dropped down on his knees to scoop out pieces of shattered rock and dirt. He was hot and furious, like a fire. I held back and did not drop down beside him because I might burn up. When the hole was scooped clean, he heaved to his feet and coughed out the words: "Try again."

He went back up the line. I raised one end of the cedar post in my arms, cradled it to my chest and dragged the heavy end into the newly enlarged hole. "Hold it straight!" He was distant again, sighting down the line. "You're leaning west!"

I leaned the post eastward. "A whisker more!" he shouted, squinting at me over the fence line. "There! Hold it! Right there!" He panted back through the prairie grass to my side, seizing the spade and shoveling dirt carefully around the post. "Steady. Don't wiggle, rascal, don't wiggle." Then once again he began hurling the steel rod for tamping, over and over.

This way, one post after another, we began to ring the corral. One afternoon when the posts were in solid, he stepped back and said, "I guess we are ready for wire." We drove to Englewood to the Purina Chow feed store. "You can never stop from getting cut up some," he said when we put the wire in the trailer, "but gloves help." So we started using gloves to keep the gouges in our hands to a minimum.

As it was with the posts, so it was with the wire. He pulled it out as tight as he could, using a hammer for leverage, and then commanded in my direction, "Lower, Craig, lower a half inch. Good! Drive your staple, Craig, drive it quick before I lose the tension." I took a staple from my mouth, hurrying because I could see the wire start to loosen even as I was fumbling to get the staple in place. Then I drove it solid, pinching the wire into the dry cedarwood. "Here, Craig, here." He approached me with another hammer. "Use the one with the better balance. That old hammer is too heavy at the business end. Too heavy, even for me. Use this one. Okay? Let's keep going!"

Through brush, rock, grasses, over the irrigation ditches, it was always the same: "Down the post, Craig, it looks to be a horsehair higher than the one just above. "Down the wire a tad, rascal, and you'll make a good line." "Raise the strand, Craig, raise it, say, a turkey feather and the strands will be even all the way. No! No! Too much. Okay! There!" When he used words that didn't quite work, like "turkey feather," I knew he was feeling good, and I smiled just a little bit.

"Take an axe to that elm in your way, Craig, take an axe to the elm! It is hardly worth the wood in it . . . too soft for posts and too small for winter fires. Don't worry about cutting elms, Craig, take it out. Cedar will last for years and makes good posts, but not elms." I hammered away at elm brush with a hand axe. "You've got it now, Craig, I think you have got it!"

Of course, it was Frank, Erik, and Don who were biggest and strongest and did most of the fence work, but I helped on those days when Frank was studying or Erik was working over on the other side by himself. In the fading light one dusky evening of midsummer, the four of us stood looking over a line of posts and the newly strung wire that would make a corral for our someday horses. Four strands of barbed wire ringed the area, poles were used in places needing special strength, and there was a pole gate that swung on fine black hinges. The strands of wire were dead-even the same distance between all strands all the way around. It looked the picture of care. "Well, I think that is all right," he said.

"Really good fence," I said. I was proud of him and us. But it was an awkward moment, somehow. He knew my intention, but he was too modest a man to go to praise for something he himself had done.

"Well," he said, pulling out a handkerchief to mop his brow. "Maybe. Maybe not. But it will hold a horse, I should think." He was picking up tools. "What you want, I think, boys," he paused, looking for the right words, "is that fifty years from now, long after you're gone—well, you won't be gone, but I will—fifty years from now, someone will sight along these posts and take some comfort. There is something pleasing to the eye about one long clean line of wire. A straight line through the waggle of trees and ditches can sing. Just when everything else seems to be haywire, somebody may come along here and say, 'Boy, look at the care in that fence.'"

I wasn't listening as well as I should have because I was having a hard time imagining what it would be like fifty years in the future when he would be gone. I didn't want to think about him being gone, ever, and I moved over close beside him and took hold of his arm. He was just trying to make me feel okay, even after I bragged about the fence. We didn't very often talk about how well we did something, and I had crossed a line. I held on to his upper arm with both my hands and looked up into his eyes. He looked down and smiled. "I'll bet dinner's ready," he said, and pulling his arm into the air dragged me toward the house where there was a yellow light in the kitchen window.

I was trotting along beside him when he said: "'Haywire'? Did I say that? What in the world do you suppose is haywire?"

"Good to keep the hay from getting out," said Erik, who was walking in beside us. Frank was there too. He chuckled.

"Yes," said Don, "I suppose." His mind was drifting off, wandering. He had a habit of trying to piece out where words came from or who invented certain tools or why roads crossed the mountain where they did or what it was like in winter in the old mining towns of the early West. "Maybe we ought to look up 'haywire,'" he said. We came out from under the cottonwoods near to the back door of the house where we could smell hamburgers sizzling. It was my favorite smell.

"It could be that when you loose a bail of hay and let the wire go, it jumps and tangles and spreads out every which way," Frank offered. It was true that wire taken off of bales of hay sometimes springs out wickedly and bites.

"Could be," he said, as he opened the door and we clomped noisily in onto the hard floors.

"Well, boys!" My mother was cheerful as we thumped inside. Before we could look for the dictionary she said: "Fence finished? You got it done?"

"Yes," said Erik. "We sure did. And it looks okay."

"Hurrah!" said my mother. "Now go wash your hands. A little soap wouldn't hurt." We were not paying attention to the soap at all, and all four of us had already been pushing into our places around the dinner table. But we didn't make it. "Really, I mean it. A little soap would not spoil your day the least little bit. You will be surprised!" I hung my head and filed back out of the dining room toward the bathroom. "And rinse your hands before you use the towels! That won't hurt either!"

She must have known we were going to finish the fence. It was not every night we could afford hamburgers, but there they were. She liked to do them with mashed potatoes and canned green peas. Don made a little pond in my potatoes to spoon in a pool of hot hamburger juice. "More, please," I said, and he ladled another spoonful so that the juice ran down the sides of the mashed potatoes like red molten lava down a white mountain. It was my favorite food except for steak, of course, but steak was only for birthdays, so this was the next best of all the things in the world to celebrate with.

"There's dessert coming," she said, "for my fence men. So, boys, you don't have to eat all the mashed potatoes in one bite."

9.

Man Training

AFTER WE GOT THE FENCE BUILT, Erik went out and got a sixteen-hand-high bay gelding that he called Captain. Frank went out and got a slick-looking black mare with a pretty white blaze down her nose; he called her Chita. So we were into the horse business. Every morning, and every night, they had to be fed. This was "chores." Chores were a mark of manhood. Farm boys did chores, which meant that not many of them could do football or basketball or play, in general, because they had already started real life. In the afternoons, after school, they slopped hogs or hayed or milked. We did not have a milk cow, which meant we were not actually the real thing, and besides my father was an engineer who went to work in the city, so we could never quite be the real thing, but I still did a lot of chores. That year at the grange raffle I bought two tickets and won the grand prize, which was a baby pig. For a while, therefore, I was a pig farmer. Since I was afraid of horses, which were higher, heavier, and stubborner than I, with a tendency to step on a person's foot or throw a person off— I weighed about sixty-five pounds—I concentrated on my pig. Compared to a horse, this was a prestige loss but a practical gain, since there is nothing to love, whatsoever, about a pig. Pigs don't hug like horses, or wrestle like dogs. It is just a plain fact that rubbing noses with a pig is dangerous. On the other hand, there is not much work to do in the one-pig business. Just take him his afternoon garbage and he's in heaven. So this pig and I did not become a personal number. He was ham and bacon from the start. You can't think like that with a horse.

Pretty soon, from somewhere, a pair of ducks came to live in our corral, and they nested in the grass by the ditch and six weeks later we had some ducklings. So I was a pig-and-duck man. My stronger, meaner, and more courageous brothers did nothing but waste money on their practically useless horses, while my pig was fattening and my ducks were increasing. I was prospering in a way that would make the president of the United States proud of young America. A pig does not have the status of a horse but is more useful from a strictly monetary point of view. Then one day I noticed that I had fewer baby ducks. Each day there was one or two less. Then I saw the ducklings in the pen with the pig and knew the sad story: the pig would as soon eat ducklings as garbage. This was bad for the pig, because ducklings are cuter and the pig was not anybody's sentimental favorite. We went to talk to Darryl Bartleme's dad down by the end of Savage's big wheatfield. Darryl said his father "knew how to do that slaughtering; they did that all the time."

When the time came, they didn't make me hold the rifle. I just put wood on the fire under the barrel for lowering the carcass into boiling water. I heard the shot and saw the skinning and all that. But I didn't have to learn like I was ever going to have to do it again. There was not much chance of winning two grange raffles in one lifetime, and I sure wasn't going to go into the pig business on purpose because of the simple fact that pigs eat ducklings. It wasn't too long before we ate the pig.

One day in the corral I fell off Captain, the big horse. He stood about sixteen hands, and it was a long way down. While I was tumbling headfirst over his shoulder and under his belly, I had plenty of time to worry about dying. The splat on the ground did not hurt so bad, but I hunkered down, trembling and rolling around, sucking air like I could die anyway. If I did not die from the blow to my head, it would be from sucking such big gulps of dust. Along came my two brave brothers and escorted me back to the horse and flung me back up there so that I would not grow up afraid. They were too late. I was already afraid. But this is how you make men. If someone is afraid, some other, bigger person just says, *No, not really, you're not afraid,* and puts the afraid person up on the horse again, even if the afraid person is glibbering and gibbering. After a while I was too tired to care if I did die or ever did live to be a hero or any such thing, so I relaxed and then they let me down. Captain and I were more or less okay after that. I was still growing and he was not, and it did not take too many years before I could look him eye to eye. This helps when you're training to be superior, which I was just beginning to get the hang of.

At school I was practicing swaggering, with my hips swinging back and forth when I walked—like the Littleton high school basketball star Terry Crandall—but my mother put the kibosh on swaggering and said it was not helpful when I was just toting water buckets out to the barn. So I had to practice superior so other people would know but my mother wouldn't. I started in my head, lying under the cottonwoods, daydreaming.

When my mother's weeds were pulled and her trees were watered, when Erik's fence was strung and my homework was done, my natural habitat was down at the prairie-dog town in the mud cliffs by the Big Bend. There was a little dog village down there. A person who was a natural could scout down along the buckbrush by the ditch to about fifty yards from where the dogs were carrying on, running along the cliffs or popped up out in the open, sunning. Then a real mountain man could sink down into the stalk grass by the edge of Savage's wheat and belly forward through the tall grass.

It's not that easy: chin above the dirt, one leg slides forward, then the other, arms out front like a giant salamander. It is slow and hard on a man's neck. I never liked slow all that much, and after a while my neck was killing me. There was always an urge to raise my head to look above the grass to see if the dogs saw me. But if I did then they would, and that would be that. Sometimes I could stand the pain long enough to get to within about seventy-five feet of where they were playing. Then I would lie in the powdered dust and be at home. Wind in the trees, sun on my face, the smell of earth and alfalfa and dry wood. The dog town was built into the face of sheer mud cliffs above the dry canal. There were major dog highway intersections, right turn up to the wheat where there was the best dog-sunning, left turn down to the swing of the great ditch beneath the cottonwoods where there were the best dry leaves and shade, or maybe straight along the cliff to the next dog settlement. "Good morning, Mrs. Gray Nose, how's the little dogs?" "Okay, Mrs. Flop Ear, but I think they could be playing hooky down at the Big Bend." "You don't say. Don't that beat all, how kids will lie around in the sun when they could be working for the whole dog-goned family." I thought I probably had the makings to be a writer, if I could go on thinking up good lines like that. But then being a writer was not one of the options that was much approved at our dinner table, so I only did it in my head when I was out on my own.

After a while, my neck would get too stiff from peering through the tops of the grasses and I got wiggly. Soon as I did that, Mrs. Gray Nose would stand up, whistle, and send the whole colony plummeting toward safety. I stood up, brushed off the twigs and dirt, and headed home to pull weeds or fix fence or some other unnatural labor for the whole dog-goned family.

Water does not run in Colorado irrigation canals year-round as it might in Seattle or New York or some of those other places. We had water in the big ditch for a month or two and then the canal went dry, leaving a few bewildered trout in pools so that small boys could run round and round and leap in after them. Neither Erik nor I had ever seen anybody cut a fish up, so we did not know what to do when we caught one, and we did not go that far. Mostly we just left them on the sand, which was probably not very smart. You'd expect more from boys that were doing okay in school, but school did not say anything about what to do with dead fish.

After that, when the pools went dry and the sand was clear, Erik started to train me to be a horse person. We rode Captain and Chita down in there and galloped full steam, hell-bent for leather, chasing Indians and passing the mail from one expert pony express rider to the next. *It is not good,* said Erik, when we'd get past the Big Bend and all the way nearly to Hap Tanner's, *to run horses to a white lather; they could catch cold, or get crumpled with gullet goiter.* We reined up and walked them back toward the broad sand at the Big Bend by the prairie-dog town. Then we wrestled on horseback.

Bareback, this is tricky. Leaning away, squeezing with my legs, I could either fall over backward or, reaching for Erik, get pulled over forward. Bad either way. The whole thing never lasts more than about a minute before someone's horse takes off for the hills or the loser ends belly up in the sand. Erik was a better rider than I and he would have liked to practice horse wrestling on Frank, but since Frank was mostly home improving his mind, Erik was left with the little kid. Once in a while when he might be weakening because of his asthma, or just recovering from the flu or scarlet fever or something he could not control, I got lucky and dragged him off his horse into the sand. This made me feel bad because we both knew that since he was bigger and better, he should have won and it was just an accident. So I said that, and he said, "No, you did good," and we rode on down the ditch looking for something better to happen.

In general, it was not smart to get Erik unhappy since he was in charge more or less of all free time, and if he did not want to do something, then something was not going to be done. I would have to wait until the right moment to suggest wrestling on the front lawn, or shooting baskets, or anything like that, and usually he would say no, he had to be studying bridles in the Miller's Stockman catalogue, or he was needing help fixing the corral, or he was using the wood lathe to make a table leg, something like that. I noticed it was wisest not to irritate any older person because then that person would never want to do anything fun. Old people generally have a lot to worry about. *Develop your own inner resources,* my mother urged me, like a broken record, when I was moping around trying to avoid fixing fence or pulling weeds. This advice seemed pretty easy to her. But my inner resources were always less advanced than those of at least the other four members of my family, so no one was ever much impressed with my suggestions. As it turned out, as a small person I could either be on my own, or if I wanted to do something with someone else, wait for an old person to suggest it. That was usually Erik. If it was a suggestion from my mother, 50 percent of the time it had to do with the dishes or weeds in the asparagus. The other 50 percent was going to be good, like Monopoly or a book, but these averages are not good when the penalty for asking the question could be as severe as weeds. If it was my father, he was kind and decent and honorable and all that, but his suggestions ran to rechecking my spelling words, or picking up in the basement, or cleaning the manure out of the corral. One he liked best was volunteering to help someone else out. He said this was sure to make me feel better. Which it did when I ever thought of it first, but somehow someone else was always thinking of me volunteering for them before I did, and just when I was planning on going to inspect the squirrels at the Big Bend, or when I was about to practice my outside, one-handed jump off the ring on the telephone pole. *It's a hard life,* my mother said. I don't know how she knew that since she had so much volunteer help.

As a trainer, my brother Frank was about as kind a man as there could be. There was not a mean bone in him. But he was the oldest, and this is a serious burden. He had to be the flag carrier. He had to be the grade getter. He had to get into Princeton. That, I can tell you, was a great gain for the whole family. Once my parents got over worrying about how smart at least *somebody* in the house was, it was easier on me and Erik. Frank did a lot of things first, and he had to do them right. He had the first girlfriend. Her name was Anne. She may have been a nice person, but Anne caused a heck of a sickness in our house. Frank moped around as if he had a high fever and lost interest in anything but the telephone. He even forgot to save money. This was almost like a squirrel giving up on nuts. He just lost himself— where he came from, where he was going—and started buying milk shakes in the afternoons at the Littleton Creamery for the woman who was causing his disease. It does not take too much intelligence to see the life-threatening danger in all this, so I vowed never to talk to Anne on the phone myself.

Frank also had the first shoulder pads for football and had to learn how to be a second-string guard and sit on the bench during big games. He was gangly and not that fast. Running was not his best thing. My mother said second string was character-building. She said, *We all have to learn to not play as much as we have to learn to play.* So we were proud of Frank because he learned how to not play quite a lot. He wanted to be good. But he was not fast, and just wanting to be fast does not help a person actually be fast.

He had one day of glory, though. Even better than getting into Princeton, to my thinking. In baseball season Frank was an outfielder. He was not fast, but he could catch the ball. That first summer he was playing in American Legion ball with one of the teams from Littleton, and they had made it all the way to the state tournament in Pueblo. In the bottom of the last inning, with nobody on base, Frank came up to bat. Things looked pretty dismal. Frank was middle down in the batting order and not what you would call the expected savior. He had a level swing, all right, but his knees pointed together, and sometimes his feet went one way and his shoulders the other. Not that any of that mattered. He was ours. He had on a clean white uniform, red letters spelling out VALORE'S HARDWARE, Littleton's finest, across his chest, a ball cap pulled snug over his eyes. He stood at the plate, staring at the pitcher like a warrior with a club. He looked so serious that Aunt Betsy started laughing. "He looks so cross," she said. "Is that a frown or a growl?"

"It's a frowl," said Erik solemnly. Betsy threw back her head and laughed right in the middle of all those people in the stands. Then we all started chuckling. We almost lost track of the balls and strikes, we were all laughing so hard.

"What is the count?" asked my mother. "Two strikes? Oh, no. Come *on*, Frank. Come *on!*"

Two strikes and no balls. The frowl got worse. Frank was in a hole. By now, no one really thought that Littleton had a chance. Then, on the next pitch, Frank swung the bat and hit the thing. The ball took off over the first baseman's head by a mile. Frank took off for first, arms flying. The ball kept on going and fell in between the center and right fielder and rolled toward the fence. Frank spindled around first and headed for second. He was moving all the body parts and dirt was kicking up and the wind was blowing, but with all that commotion he was not gaining nearly enough real estate. The right fielder ran for the ball, picked it up, and whipped around, throwing hard toward second. Frank came around windmilling toward the bag while we were screaming from the stands.

"Hurry! Frank! *Hurry!*" yelled Aunt Betsy who was a Sewall descendant and always said things politely.

My mother, who must have imagined the Red Sea collapsing, simply yelled, "Run!" as if that might not yet have occurred to him.

Then Frank left the ground and, like a crane coming in for a landing, began the glide through the air toward second base. At the same time, here came the ball bouncing in from right field. There was a mighty crash and dust flew and bodies rolled in the dirt. The world came to a halt and for a moment nobody or nothing moved. Then there was Frank lying flat on his back, hugging second base to his chest like a long-lost physics textbook, frowling from ear to ear. "SAFE!" yelled the umpire after an ungodly pause, and my mother screamed and Aunt Betsy screamed and I screamed.

. Erik said, accurately enough, "Good hit." It was extra words for him. He could have just said "Good."

What with all the commotion at second base, Littleton now had a man in scoring position. The rest was easy. The next person up was so inspired that he got a hit too, driving Frank all the way around third into home. Frank scored the winning run. At the end of the game there was a big crowd of parents milling around and everybody said that Frank had saved the day. As a family, then, we had to decide whether to go for milk shakes. This was a red-letter deal. No award, for a Barnes, marked a celebration higher than a chocolate malt or a shake. But shakes cost twenty-five cents and the malt was a nickel more and it was already four-thirty in the afternoon and my mother said, "We have already spent this month's mad money on gasoline just to come all the way to Pueblo; we'd better go home." We headed out to squeeze into the old black Chevy.

But when we got in, Aunt Betsy said, "Well, you can't just drive home, not like that. Not after Frank's hit. I'll pay for it." She insisted we find a creamery and when we did, Frank had a malt and the rest of us had shakes because it was Aunt Betsy's money. They were the coolest, sweetest shakes anybody could ever remember. Victory shakes for the conquerors from Littleton.

Driving back to Littleton in the '41 Chevy, two hours with me, Erik, Aunt Betsy, and my mother, Frank was a hero. He showed how heroes can be modest in the face of extreme praise, and I tried to learn that, too.

10.

The Boy Who Would Be King

"WHEN A PERSON IS OLD ENOUGH to notice, he may get the impression that he is just a little different. Could be bad, could be good," Erik said, "but once in a while difference runs in our favor. For instance, we call Don by his first name." This was a permission, as best as we could tell, granted by the authorities to only a very few special people. We boys knew we were being honored. Kids who called their parents "Father" and "Mother" were usually city people, government people, or Republicans. "You can spot a city person quicker than a frog in the bathtub by the use of the word 'Daddy,'" said my friend Daryl. So, in general, to avoid normalcy and ordinariness, we did not do what everyone else did and called our father by his real name. This permission was a gift. We knew it, and we treasured it. At the same time, most folks would have said that we showed a lack of respect, or maybe that our father was trying to lower himself to our level, not respecting himself.

"Could be right," Don would say, thinking about it, "so we ought not make a show of it." Making a show was not his style. And, of course, when it really came down to respect, there was never any doubt about who was the supreme authority at our place. The one and only day I ever stood up to him, I cowered and trembled and nearly did myself in.

Barneses were always being careful, measuring this or that. I don't mean pots and pans. I had no idea about cups and tablespoons or quarts or pints—kitchen things. But I knew about gallons, because we carried gallons of water in buckets to the barn, and tons of hay in a stack and acres of alfalfa and cubic feet of water through the headgate. My father liked numbers and he liked the ruler and a long steel tape. He liked corners that were tight and schedules and promises that were kept, and didn't like cloth tapes that stretched, the same way he didn't like people who stretched or pretended they didn't mean what it sounded like they meant.

My two older brothers were good with tools and liked numbers, too. Erik worked on the wood lathe for hours at a time, skinning a table leg out of a cedar post, and Frank fed on calculus and trigonometry like a calf loose in the alfalfa. They were pretty close to where they were natural, which was natural doers, workers, get-it-done people. They knew the dangers of too much carrying on, or too much hanging around thinking things over.

I couldn't help it, though. I liked big questions. And I liked kings and capes and trumpets. Drama was big-time in my book. Sometimes I went through a whole day pretending I was acting in a movie: *the boy climbs to the top of the stack. The boy throws a heavy forkload of hay to the ground. Do you see that strong swing there, pitchfork through the air in an easy arc of natural grace? Now see: the boy has his face to the wind, scanning the horizon for signs of a change in the weather. He is a son of the prairie, this boy; a true pioneer, a gentle boy of great wisdom.* There was some of my Grandmother Schellenberg's Oregon opera in me. It was a secret, though. If ever I had let on to anyone I was going through this grandeur when I was only standing on a no-good haystack pitching hay to the sheep, they would have had me committed. But they didn't know how bad it really was. Some days I was even unreliable. One day Erik caught me at it, mumbling up there on the stack. "When a person starts talking to himself, it is the first sign of insanity," he said.

"Yeah," I said, "but if a person does not talk at all, his tongue will freeze to the top of his mouth. He could die."

"Better to freeze your tongue than to go stir-crazy."

I jumped way off into the air, black boots landing in the dust with a crash, stumbling wildly in his direction until I careened into him. "Ooops, sorry."

"Yeah, sorry, smorry," he said. But he was half laughing and I was half laughing. We went on with the business of feeding and watering the stock and he forgot that I was talking to myself.

He did not know, though, how close he came to the mark. I was up there acting most of the time. Or I was working my way forward through the buckbrush, belly to the ground, closing in on the buffalo herds of yesterday. But now, since the open range was filling up with people and some of them, like my brother, could even hear me talking up there on the haystack, I would have to be more careful. From then on, I played all these movies in my head very quietly.

We were so far from kings and queens and royal deeds in Arapahoe County that if one of Shakespeare's heroes had come walking down the ditch road, somebody would have called the sheriff. One time a city friend came to visit for the day. He was not good for much in the way of fixing fence or watering chickens, so my mother said it would be okay to make up a play to perform in the house. We summoned the family to be there at four in the afternoon to see the latest heroic adventures of Sinbad the Sailor. During the performance I leapt over the couch and swirled my towel cape in the air, soaring through the most death-defying life leaps. My friend and I had brilliant sword fights and saved wretched maidens, golden treasure, and a sacred white calf, all right there in the living room in the course of ten minutes. The audience of four was mildly impressed.

My mother said she was sure that I would get a lot of pleasure in my life out of my interest in drama. The tone she used was the one she used when she was admitting that there would be certain medicinal uses for alcohol, maybe in Europe, maybe when you were trying to save a dying man from freezing in a blizzard. Drama, like alcohol, would be good someday if I was stuck on a desert island. My father smiled but didn't say anything. He and my brothers went back to the serious consideration of problems for which Sinbad the Sailor was not the solution.

Other people saw an ordinary summer's drought and I saw a drought like no one had ever seen, time out of mind, even before the Indians, one of a kind. Not a big difference, maybe, just that I always wanted to put a spin on it, wanted to see it larger, wanted there to be something important even about a rainless June. One time a rainbow pointed down into the back alfalfa. It was just when the sun was headed west over the high peaks and golden rays lay long and low through the cottonwoods. The mist from a finished cloudburst was steaming up off the fields right where the rainbow came down, but there was no pot of gold in our pasture. "Nope," said Erik who went on reading saddle catalogues, "of course not."

Frank, seeing my face, said: "You're not likely to ever see a real pot of gold, not really. Pots of gold are mostly in books from old stories in Europe. It may have a symbolic meaning, though." And then he went wisely back to his trigonometry. I just stood there at the window, watching the steam rise up out of the field, wondering. My brothers asked me, finally, what I was doing and I said, "Oh nothing, oh, no, I'm coming. I'll be right there." I did not know myself what I was doing. But always there was this attraction, especially to things that caught the light or that rode the wind or that were far away. I never could figure out why things were as they were.

A person couldn't measure my questions. No one could put a steel tape to a rainbow. On the other hand, thinking about those big questions usually left me working on the fence like a sort of zombie. "Craig just doesn't think about what we are doing," said Erik one night when we were talking about a day that we had spent hoisting rails and spiking them to the new corral gate. "He doesn't see the obvious things." That day he had been searching around in the grass for a hammer, which was lying beside me, and I just watched him search, waiting for him to say, "Have you seen the hammer?" Then I gave it to him. Anybody with a right mind would have handed him the hammer before the question, so he wondered where in the world I was in my head. I was out in the wheat field, more than likely, wondering what the magpies were doing bunching on the wind over the alfalfa. Or I was wondering if this fence was like the fences of old, like they built in the time of the Dry Creek gold rush, or that they leaned against when Wyatt Earp had his famous shoot-out.

When Erik made that comment about me not seeing the real things around me, I felt all pinched up inside, because I wanted to be a good worker, like him and Frank and my father, and I did not know what was wrong with me. I thought I could overcome it with more effort. They were all kind enough about it; they thought it was just the normal conduct of an undisciplined young person, like a calf that is not quite trained to lead. I worried that if I did not get it right, they would treat me like some horse who could never be broke to pull the buggy and would just give up on me. *Not to worry*, they said, *if I would concentrate better, I would learn to be a good worker.* Not to worry, not to worry. But the more they said it, the more I realized I had a lot to worry about.

I imagined that all the rest of them had already overcome whatever the disease was I had in my head, the fever of questions, the fascination with thunderheads or powerful floods, or the powerful sadness. So whenever the disease hit me, I tried to override it. One fall afternoon I was lying on the warm earth, feeling the hot dirt through my shirt, feeling blessed by it, smelling the dry stalk grass that was already curling up for winter. There is a way that dry grass smells when you put your head down into it that is clean and sweet and feels like home. But then I began thinking about the acres of hay we had cut that summer and the bales of hay that were in, measurements for all that, and the water that it took to irrigate those acres, the acre-feet per year. I remembered that everything comes down to measurement, even the time that I spent in the fields, looking things over, or lying face in the grass. I remembered how my father did not want me wasting time and that I knew the rules, especially for measuring time spent on something as inconsequential as the sweet dry smell of fading summer grass. So I went on in to get to work.

I memorized some simple lessons. *When they work, I work. When they're happy, I'm happy. When they want to play, I want to play.* I tried to become as indistinguishable from other Barneses as one shaft of wheat is from another. But one day the situation got very sticky. Erik was talking to Mike Cervi, from over across the wheat field. Mike was a sort of neighbor and a horseman, like Erik. They were standing by the corral fence, sharing stories about horses. Mike said he was looking for a fast horse. Erik was wise, or silent, which we Barneses took for the same thing, while Mike was talking about all the sales and auctions he had gone to. I don't know how they got onto the subject of me. Maybe it was when Mike asked whether I was going to get a horse, too. I overheard Erik say: "Well, Craig is different. He's a thinker."

It hit me pretty hard. The immediate reason behind that statement was a pheasant egg I had found alongside an abandoned nest in the deep alfalfa. I had brought it back to the house and with instructions from *Boy's Life,* poked tiny holes into each end and blew the egg dry so I could keep it. It was beautiful and small, green, fragile. I liked to just hold it, or to put it on the shelf by my bed and look at it. Then around the corner of the chicken shed I heard Erik explain to Mike, "Craig is different." Erik was decent about it. "Some people just are interested in the small stuff," he explained gently, and Mike took it in, trying to understand how some people could be interested in something as inconsequential as a pheasant egg.

"I could crush that damn egg just like that," said Mike, laughing quietly.

"Yeah, you could," said Erik, "but you wouldn't want to do that, not really. There wouldn't be any sense in it." They both stood there, staring at the ground, trying to fathom the boy who liked pheasants' eggs. "And he can get mad," said Erik. "He has a temper. Then I don't know how it would come out. He can get real mad."

So there I was laid bare like a plucked chicken. It is hard to imagine three worse things. I liked things delicate and inconsequential, I liked things pretty, and I got mad or lost my temper enough so that Erik had even noticed. It seemed to me that I had been branded. After that I made very little fuss about my pheasant's egg. I tried to stay a true Barnes. Back before I had that interest, I thought, life had been easier. Now it was useful to disguise the fact that I liked things like a pheasant's egg or a wildflower. I never said anything about it. I even liked to sing and spread my arms and twirl in the wind when it was blowing leaves under the cottonwoods, but I never did that when anyone else was around. I liked to watch the prairie dogs play and I liked to warm up in the hot sun on dry earth, lying in tall dry stalk grass under green cottonwoods. I really was like Ferdinand the Bull, just as my father said, and I could sit for hours under waving branches, watching clouds go by, waiting for a bird to come hopping through the grass.

"Craig can think like a horse better than anyone if he wants to," said Erik one day, trying to be helpful, turning the whole thing around, meaning high praise. He said that a person who watches birds and squirrels can get to know how they think. And a person who thinks like a horse can be very useful, if he wants to be. It was true; I had a pretty good idea how to read the signs. So did he, of course, but he was trying to be nice. What he meant was there is a way, for sure, that a horse turns a half shoulder away, saying, *Forget it, cowboy, I'm on lunch break*. But Erik knew, and I knew too, that sometimes a horse will lift a head to look you over and just by the softness in his eye you can tell he doesn't really mean with his mind what he is saying with his shoulder. Especially if it's only a half turn; in that case the beast is really ready for more conversation. Then you can work your way up to him, even in the open, just by pretending to have the same grazing schedule, taking your time, wandering close and then far until, after he is through worrying, you can just slide an arm over his neck and bring him in.

"Good enough," said my father one day after I had spent the whole morning out in the field grazing alongside Chita, working into her confidence. Trying to catch her in a new way, I had spent that time on my hands and knees, head in the grass, pretending to be grazing, getting the feel of her jitters or her resistance until she got to be curious and actually came over to see what this small boy was up to. Then I brought her in with a glow on my face.

"Too slow," said Erik, who by then had forgotten that he was trying to be nice to me. A person cannot be nice to another person forever. He had been waiting all morning for me to get done so we could fix fence together. It is just possible that I knew that, and maybe that was why I took so long to catch the horse. I am not admitting that outright, but it is just possible.

"Well, it took time, but he showed a lot of patience," said my father.

"Still pretty slow for any practical purpose," said Erik.

I plodded around the house. "There's work to do," Erik said, handing me a hammer and a coffee can full of nails, "and only doin' it will get it done." I guess he figured I was out there just smelling the grass. I actually was perfecting a very natural new way to catch a horse, an Indian way, a true American way, a cowboy way that he could use if he was stranded in the wide-open spaces without a rope. This was not avoiding work. This was near genius. I maybe even said that.

He said, "By the time you got that horse the Indians would have had you for lunch." He had been waiting for me for about three hours.

"Another day of forced labor," I said.

"Only doin' it will get it done," he repeated.

Well, that was that. In Arapahoe County, great wranglers' careers began and ended just because there was wire to stretch, or hay to put up, or there could be any other old penny-ante deal to keep a small boy from dreaming he's a star.

"You'll be a star someday," said my father comfortingly, "just not today. Even great stars have to start in the corral." He was laughing softly.

"What?" I asked gloomily. I did not know why he was laughing.

"Nothing," he said. "You just have to get used to it. Get out your school book tonight. Look at that mythic man cleaning the stables." He chuckled some more. "He cleans and cleans. For seven days he cleans, or something like that. I think our Craig has stumbled into the Augean stables."

"Yeah," I said.

"Well, it won't hurt you," he said. "It won't hurt you to clean the stables. Today it's fence, but it's all the same as stables. That's what you have to do to become like Ulysses."

He was still chuckling as I went over to help Erik with the wire. I was maybe too slow to be a real cowboy, or too fragile, or maybe not tough enough even to face real life, like shooting the pig, or letting things die when they have to die. So Erik was becoming a real horseman, and I was wondering what it would take to ever be a star.

It was not that selfish, really. Frank was a star. He got that game-winning hit in Pueblo, and he got straight As in school. Erik was so admirably honest it hurt, and I could tell this was easier for him than it was for me. He would say to me, "I don't want to do that right now," or he would tell Mike Cervi his horse was out "again, for the third time this month," or he would tell Mrs. Post, his teacher, "I am not going to sing because I can't."

I would have said, if it had been me, "Well, okay, sure I'll sing," and then I would have hung my head and done something like trying to sing, even if I didn't know how. So Erik was truly honest, and I was more or less trying to be, as long as I could be liked and keep friends with everyone.

Then he said to me on that particular day, handing me the nails, "Only doin' it will get it done."

For some reason, I lost it. The hammer and nails were still in my arms. I dropped the can of nails from about three feet off the ground. The can bounced and nails scattered every which way.

"You didn't have to do that," said Erik, fixing me in the eye with a steady glare.

"Doesn't matter to you what I do," I said. "I guess you gave me the nails. I can do with 'em what I want." He stared at me. I felt misunderstood, ignored, and overworked. I kicked the coffee can as hard as I could. It sailed off the ground and crashed against the side of the hill where the ditch road was. Nails scattered all throughout the tall prairie grass. It would take forever to find them.

"You didn't have to do that, either," said Erik with disgust.

My father chose that moment to stop spading the irrigation ditch and came over to where we stood glaring at each other. He did not have a shirt on and was tanned dark brown. The spade work was hard, and he was dripping sweat off his brow and down his copper chest.

"What's this all about?" he asked.

"Craig is being dumb," said Erik.

"My nails. My work. I can do what I want," I spit back at him.

"Best pick up the nails," said my father, "and get back to work." He turned to walk away.

I lost myself. "And what if I don't?"

My father stopped in his tracks and turned around. He looked me dead in the eye.

"Don't ever talk to me like that," he said slowly. "Go. Go to your room. Write an apology. Don't come out until you can live with civilized people."

My knees were shaking. I put down the hammer very carefully, picked up the coffee can, and started to look for nails in the grass.

"Go," he said, "to your room."

I put down the coffee can. I went to my room. This had not happened before. My will against his. I sobbed and sobbed. The afternoon dragged on. I went to sleep and woke up, exhausted, scoured out, clean and dead inside. I got out a pencil and a piece of paper. I wasn't sure what an apology was more than a simple "I'm sorry," so I thought I had better do something more. I wrote about what went wrong, why I had got off-track, and what would keep me out of trouble in the future.

RULES
Fix fence for Erik.
Don't kick the nails.

That was all I could think of to make out of fence and nails, so I started on all the dinner-table rules that I had heard a hundred times.

Measure your thoughts. Think before you speak.
Develop your inner resources.
If you sleep out at night under the cottonwoods,
*   do not run potato races in your sleeping bag.*
Don't feed the dogs at the table.
Don't get angry. Not ever. About anything.
Don't skin rabbits in the kitchen.
Don't store dead skunks in the basement.

I was starting to feel better. So I wrote:

Don't hug brothers. Ever.
Don't hug calves, either, or chickens, but
*   especially not pigs.*

After a long time, I opened the door to my room and looked around. There was no one in the house. I walked over to the back door and heard hammering in the corral. I walked out the door and slowly toward the sound. It seemed like the whole family had some excuse to be out in the corral. They were all there, pounding and hammering on something, at least until I dragged up. Then they all stopped.

"Oh, hi, Craig," said Erik. He sounded like he was not still mad. But I did not say anything.

I gave my father the paper. He read what I had written and almost smiled, but I couldn't tell for sure. "It's not an apology," he said, "but pretty close."

He handed the paper to my mother, who was pruning some wild rosebushes that grew outside the fence along the irrigation ditch. "That's good," she said firmly. She folded the paper and gave it back to my father, and then straightened up with the pruning shears in one hand and looked off toward the mountains. I thought maybe she was checking the weather or something. "You know, Donald," she said slowly, "I think this might be a good night for a movie." Her eyes were shining. I stood there motionless because I knew then that judgment was being passed. Don looked at her, and he knew and we all knew that we could not afford movies all that often and that movies were for times when we really needed a lift, so he was getting a sign.

"That would be a very good idea," said Frank, sensing that something was needed. He seemed like he was not mad either. "Maybe even," he said with a smile, "with a stop off afterwards for a chocolate shake. I could pay for mine."

"Me too," said Erik.

"Could be," said Don, and that cinched it.

So that night we saw Laurence Olivier play Shakespeare's *Henry V*. He swaggered and strutted around the make-believe Globe Theater like a great king. This was my kind of king. "Once more unto the breach, noble English! Once more unto the breach!" Yeah! I thought. Once in the middle of the movie when the king was in his castle, he lifted his jeweled crown from his head and twirled it through the air. It sailed about ten feet and came down perfectly, skewered on the back post of the hallowed throne of England.

"Wow," I said as we drove home. "What a great king!"

"The crown can be heavy sometimes," said my father. "It was not so easy being king. But yes, that was an all right king."

I didn't care if anyone thought the crown could be heavy. The way Henry swirled it through the air I thought was the way a person should be king. "Can we read Shakespeare again some time?" I asked.

"Might be," said my father.

"Sometime," said my mother. I was slowly becoming aware that not everyone liked Shakespeare as much as I did and not everyone wanted to be a star or even liked stars.

When we got home and the three of us were under the covers, Don came in and sat at the foot of my bed. From where he sat all three of us could hear him. He said quietly, "The question is, how can you use all that star energy, all that excitement, like Henry, to harness all that enthusiasm to something really worthwhile?"

"Because everyone can't be king," Erik said from his bed.

"Well, it would be okay to be a good king," said Don, "but it is a little late to put in your bid. Some of us were, worse luck, born into the wrong family." He wiggled his nose as he did when he teased us and smiled.

"Yeah," I said, "and probably I wouldn't like it that much."

After a while he said: "You know those rules you wrote?" I shivered. I thought that he might be angry that I had said that pigs and brothers were the same thing. I wanted to slide under the covers.

"Yeah."

"You have a flair for writing, Craigalatch. Keep it up." He stood up and came to my pillow and ruffled my hair. Then for a moment I forgot about being angry and forgot about being a star. At least I was in the family again.

"It could get worse," he said, trying to be encouraging.

"Yeah," I said, "I'm all right." He reached down and gave me a hug and I squeezed him back so hard that I might have choked him. Then he quietly left the room.

"You're not really insane," said Erik from across the room in his bed after Don had gone. "Even if you do talk to yourself. I do too, sometimes. We all do. I was just teasing."

"Yeah," I said. "I know."

Erik was okay, really. Everything was okay, I guess. Except I lay awake a long time wondering whether anyone could live like that king. Not just as king, I mean, even if a person wasn't king. I did not know anyone who would swirl his crown or his hammer or his book—whatever it was—through the air and laugh and strut and swagger and still be good. All the people I heard about who were like that were not so good. My father thought the two went together, strutting or crown swirling, and getting carried away. *That was just the moment when a boy would forget his measurements, forget the consequences,* he said. It made me sad. I felt like a rosebush that was being pruned. In a good way, I guess. But still, pruned.

"Time to prune the apple trees," my mother would say in the fall. "Before the harvest comes the pruning." It was the natural way. Boys and trees both get watered. But then they get pruned. I went to sleep wondering if there could be fruit from such a warped and spindly tree. They were all with me, and still I felt alone.

II.

One Time a Champion

WHITE IS FOR THIRD, red is for second, and blue is for first. This is normal. Purple, as everyone now knows, is the champion, the grand champion. A grand-champion ribbon is solid purple with gold lettering; there are two ribbons joined at the top under a wide purple rosette, and in the purple center, in this case, it says in capital gold letters, GRAND CHAMPION, ARAPAHOE COUNTY FAIR, 1948. There is only one such ribbon for all the fair. There was only one Grand Champion chicken.

It all started at Christmas 1947. It was Colorado plains cold. On Christmas Eve, the night before, we sang carols and lit candles in the windows in the living room, the dining room, and the two bedrooms. We ringed the inside of the house with golden light. We had already pasted up the cutouts of the Three Kings, sent to us by our ancient great-aunt, Archie, who couldn't hear and couldn't much think anymore, but was still our family's resident expert on cutouts. Throughout December a person could see Aunt Archie's cardboard camels plodding from south to north, following the star of Bethlehem across our front window toward the manger. We didn't have the right kind of window for the kings to go westward leading, like they should have, but this was not one of the details that had to be absolutely perfect. This tradition was not from the engineering side of the family. This was from the Sewall and preacher side. "It's the thought that counts," said my mother, who was the local representative of all things outside the world of engineering.

The tree was up. There had been no need for surprise since age seven when I had sneaked into the closet and found the tommy gun and then died the death of a thousand guilty criminals. We were still putting on ornaments when my mother called from the kitchen: "Don't forget the angel doll from when I was a child, boys, please." Angels and dolls, unfortunately, are mostly for girls and almost always pink. Nobody gets to be a man thinking pink. But it was Christmas and she could not help that she was a girl, so I did put that pink angel doll on the tree, a little low and toward the back.

Packages were under the tree by late afternoon. It got dark early and after dinner my mother played carols on the piano, my father sang with a honey-sweet voice, and when we ran out of songs she said with a twinkle, "Okay, boys, time for bed." She said we could go to sleep by listening to Radio City Music Hall from New York City. I lay with my head on the clean white pillow and heard the tragic tale of Tiny Tim and Bob Cratchit. Those people for sure did not live in Arapahoe County and they had uncommon troubles. I felt sorry that London, where there were kings, was just a little less advanced than Littleton.

Morning—Christmas morning—*the* morning— there were stockings to pour out on the bed, each with a shiny pocket knife, or a stapler and a box of pencils "for our diligent young speller," or a game with a steel ball that rolled around holes in a wooden box. There were candy canes and rock peppermints and an orange tangerine in the toe. After an eternal delay the elders were supposed to come in to sing "We Three Kings" and lead us to the tree lit, packages all around. And always, there was the Big Present.

The Big Present was the deal. One year, my brother Erik got six cedar fence posts, lying out on the front lawn, and then we knew he would be working on the corral for a horse. Later, he got a harness and we knew he would be getting a buggy, trying to get that horse to pull. This was a mistake, of course, because the horse was not a pulling horse and that buggy came to a quick, immediate, and tragic end wrapped around a fence post. But we did not know that at the time, so we sort of enthused and said, "Good, Erik, a buggy!" For those of us who were younger and more sensible and who did not try to change quarter horses into something that they were not, by nature, and never would be, we got things like bicycles, or a microscope for Frank, who probably because of some moral flaw was very attached to seeing little things blown up big.

The fence posts were not the best. I mean, not as a Big Present. Even Erik, who had an uncommon fondness for manual labor, which meant that he did not need games, really, in his life at all, except maybe on Sundays, and who dreamed of owning a ranch where there were only men and the world was clean and fine and nobody had to talk much, still would rather have had a present he could talk about a little. The long-term prospect of a horse was great, he was smart enough to know that, but he was also smart enough to see that first we would have to dig and chisel maybe a hundred two-foot-deep holes in the Colorado clay, and then stretch four strands of wire, and pound a whole lot of staples, all before he got a horse. The distance between posts and a horse flying like the wind along the ditch under the cottonwoods was going to be months. We had a job, that Christmas, cheering up Erik. He was not ever what you would call a greedy sort of person, too shy to ask for himself, so you didn't hear anything like a peep of discontent from him. Still, that year my mother and father and all of us were busy trying to think of a game to play with Erik, or asking if he wanted to wrestle, or do some useful thing because he liked to do useful things.

But that was before the chickens. This year, just at first light when we were still exploring the pocket knives and puzzles, when I was eating a candy cane and playing tangerine catch with Erik, we heard a knock on the window. We could barely see outside because of the frost that covered the panes, and they gave off only a kind of pale blue light. Frank started scratching at the frost. At first, he couldn't see anything out there but bright, blue cold. Then he saw my mother, a woolen scarf wrapped tight up to her ears, cold frost boiling out of her mouth. "Get dressed and crawl out the window," she whispered. "The car won't start." Her voice had shrunk like dried ice. Snow was all over the roads and fields of Arapahoe County. "We just have a little errand for Santa." She tried to smile but couldn't make her lips bend. We all three got dressed, cranked open the bedroom window, squeezed out one by one like cubes popping from the ice tray, and fell face-first into the snow. She led us away from the living-room window. "Don't look back," she said, trying to laugh, but her lips would not work. When we got to the Chevy, Don was leaning against the trunk and he was not having any more luck smiling than she was. We lined up to push until the Chevy started rolling downhill. Then small boys began peeling off like spent rocket casings, rolling into the snow gasping. After about fifty feet the engine coughed and popped and the car steamed away.

"Santa will be very grateful!" said my mother. She was still trying to laugh but nothing would make her lips move, so we walked back around the house like four little steam engines, huffing and puffing. I stood on Frank's hands and he pushed me back up through the window. An hour later, the Chevy steamed back into the driveway. There was some loud squawking in the living room and then silence. As if nothing had happened, my mother suddenly threw open the door to the bedroom and started singing "We Three Kings." The tree lights were all on, the candles were lit. The room was festive and a fire was roaring. Don was sitting on the floor in front of the burning hearth trying desperately to control two very upset chickens.

He sat with one arm around each bird, singing "We Three Kings" in the birds' ears, but it was not calming them. The rest of us stood wide-eyed, crooning, staring at the two hens squawking and flapping.

So Christmas was always the beginning of something. How to sink fence posts. How to collect stamps. How to harness a horse. For me, how to raise chickens.

It depended, they said, on how I did. If I did well, which meant that I demonstrated some sense of responsibility—considered unlikely, I could later go into large animals, raising calves and horses like my brothers. The chickens, therefore, were supposed to test a small boy's promise. If I did well, I might get permission to someday have a real animal, which was like getting permission to grow up. If I grew up, life could improve. It was not that I had a bad life; I had a perfect life, except that I was always youngest and littlest. If I could grow up, I might be older than at least somebody.

The first step was to join the 4-H club, and I did that in January 1948. We drove out to a farmhouse east on the plains in full, flat-out wheat country. As we sat in a farmer's living room, the leader went around the circle and asked each new kid to name his or her stock. Everybody had to have a stock project to be in 4-H. Somebody said pigs. Somebody said Hereford calves. Somebody said he had Arabians. One girl had a big red thoroughbred. Big stuff. When he got to me I said "Chickens."

The leader said, "How many?"

I said "Two."

The leader was a swarthy man with a sunburned face. He did not spend much time indoors, I didn't think. "How many?" he asked again, looking extremely serious.

"Two," I said, looking down. "Hens."

The girl with the big thoroughbred snickered. The 4-H leader worked his jaw, like he was trying to swallow some large piece of meat. "Next," he said without looking up.

That was it for January. I was into 4-H, but not exactly a trendsetter. The next month, February, is a bad month in mud country. Boots off at the back door. Boots to dry in the sun. Boots to scrape with a kitchen knife. And behind the scraping I still hear a persistent voice from the back door: "Must you? Don't use my good knives, boys, please!" followed by a pause and then Erik's whispered comment where he was scraping away down beside me: "I told you."

Mornings, the mud was usually frozen and okay. But regular afternoon feeding required a trek to the barn and mud again. Boots off at the back door again. Boots to scrape with a kitchen knife again. During these weeks, snow melted, softened the soil, froze, pulverized the clay, dried, then it snowed again over and over. From the perspective of a chicken farmer, February is one month that we could do without. "You can't cancel it," Erik said, "because there are too many people who have birthdays in it. They would have to be transferred to another month, and you can't do that, not really." So we had to recognize February as a sort of necessary delay, or dead time, before wheat would be showing green and the Highline Canal would fill up, maybe in March or April. Altogether we had about sixty days to wait. Erik read horse catalogues; I read County Extension manuals in the "Art and Practice of Poultry Raising" to see if I could learn the difference between a show chicken and an ordinary chicken. By County Fair time I needed to know. Come August, there would be horse races and Catch-It-Calf contests and competitions among all the stock owners in the county. Like suds are to soap, you can bet we would be at County Fair.

To fill up February, and also because I had been very responsible in feeding and watering my two hens, one day we went down to Jamison's Hatchery in Englewood and bought fifty day-old, bright yellow chicks. It was too cold to put them outside in the coop, so we put them under a lightbulb in the basement. Every morning and evening I had to change the newspaper underneath them, which would get pretty soiled in that time. Most people would think, oh boy, what a mess. Not me. That mess, newspaper and chicken mess, was my future. I got to feeling awfully good about that smell and all those little yellow balls of fluff running around peeping, stepping into the water feeder, instinctively scratching the paper as if it were dirt, trying to uncover more seed grain, starting to grow feathers. In about six weeks they were old enough to take outside. In that time, I had lost only one or two. The rest had lived. I had faithfully fed and watered and changed the paper every day. "Isn't that good, Donald?" my mother asked one evening. She called him Donald when she wanted him to agree. I knew the signal and was pleased that she was pleading my case. "Good," said my father, who was writing a chapter for a book about engineering.

On weekends, sometimes, Don could be distracted from the thin-print engineering life. One day in January he put down his paperwork and hauled in lumber and windows and nails. Evenings, he sat under the yellow lampshade and designed a coop with windows facing the south sun and six nests and a little doorway at the bottom that the chickens could use for going in and out. It took about a month for him to build and then the two Christmas hens moved in. By late February, I moved the basement chicks out into the new coop and then bought fifty more day-olds. I was now up to 102, not counting the few that I had lost. But they never asked me again at 4-H how many chickens I had. I wasn't anxious to talk about it. My two old hens were not laying. If you are in the chicken business, you are supposed to sell eggs. February and March went by and the two hens were barren. I could not tell 4-H that even the two that I had did not lay. They ate grain and water, day after day, and when the coop was ready, I went out every afternoon looking, but there was never an egg. I kept reading the County Agent's manual and trying to learn the difference between a healthy and a sick chicken and what to do to get chickens to lay eggs. My mother said, *Well, maybe they are still not used to living here. Be patient. It will all be all right when the baby chicks are old enough to lay.*

While I was reading the manual looking for a cure for barren chickens, I began to learn something else. I began to read other sections about what makes a good show chicken. I learned that a New Hampshire's neck should not have black specks, and that it is supposed to be clear red and rusty clean. I learned about how a rooster's comb is supposed to stand tall and what color red it should be and how it should fold. I learned that there is a certain purple for the New Hampshire rooster's tail, and there should not be any specks of black down his head, either. So I was thinking and learning. Short of canceling it, I did the best that could be done with February. In March, my chicks grew feathers and began spreading their wings, strutting around and flapping. They were beginning to look like real birds. Mornings and nights, before and after school, I grained them. I liked the work. Nobody else ever depended upon me like my chickens did.

Later that spring, about time for the first cutting of alfalfa, when the ditch had been running brown and full for a couple of months, that is, when irrigation summer was in full swing and the cottonwoods were green and magnificent along the canal, one of the original two red hens finally laid an egg. I was performing my evening ritual, walking along the cubicles that were optimistically described as nests, having poured water into the feeder and grain, and checking to see how everybody was doing. Then I examined the nests, because this was the most fun thing to do, even if I had been doing it for six months without result. There in the last box was a pale, brown, beautiful egg. I dropped my bucket, took the egg in both hands, and carefully cradled it back to the house. "I got an *egg!*"

There were shouts and screams of delight from my mother. "Oh, no! I don't *believe* it. Let's see!" So we had a sort of festive night, I was excused from doing the dishes, and next morning my mother wanted to know if I wanted the egg for breakfast. But I did not want to lose it, so we saved it a couple of weeks before she finally persuaded me. "You've got to eat it eventually," she said. So I did. It tasted like a normal egg. I don't know what I was expecting.

In Arapahoe County, there was snow season, melting season, the beginning of irrigation when water came into the canal, haying time, another round of irrigation and haying, and then County Fair. This was pretty much it for the year, our calendar for the Colorado prairie. After Fair was school, which, in the overall scheme of things, was only sort of a wedge between other major events of life. Then came the thinning of the leaves and snow again.

That year, 1948, it came time when the wheat was golden and the combines had come and gone, and the alfalfa was almost ready for a third cutting, and the whisper in the air was that everybody was getting ready for Fair. Erik had a new horse, a dapple gray mare. He began looking her over, rubbing her, washing her down. This was our first horse washing. Fifteen hands high of horse flesh and shampoo. My mother couldn't stop laughing. Smoky was not all that pretty a horse, if you think about long legs and well-turned shanks and the things that make for a show horse. She was good for sitting bareback because she was round with practically no backbone, but no one thought the judge would give points for the best horse to wrestle on. Still, we were hopeful. We were looking for the kind of judge my mother called "broad-minded." Really, we told her,

Smoky glitters in the sun after a shampooing. We all thought she looked fat but fine.

Erik also entered the Catch-It-Calf contest, giving him a chance to catch a live calf and keep it, which would get him started in the cattle business big-time. No one needed to say how important that was, and Erik, being the best athlete in the family, was thought to have our best chance. He would get his run on the last night of the Fair, right out there in the middle of the fairgrounds, in the rodeo ring. There would be fifty kids and twenty-five calves in a large pen, and two, three hundred people cheering, roaring when some small boy tumbled under hoof or grabbed a tail, dragging in the dirt, hanging on to his cattle future, spitting mud. It was going to be chaos in there. Only half of them could be winners, so half were going to slink home muttering, "I just couldn't get a-holt of that damn thing." I know, because a couple of years later I tried, and that is exactly what I said. Only, of course, I wouldn't say "damn," because we didn't do that.

Several days before the Fair was to begin, I went out to my flock. I knew from the manuals what I was looking for. A pair of well-matched hens, same size, same shape, same coloring, and no flecks on the neck. Good feet. Good combs. I had a flock of young ones to choose from. These were the birds that were started in the basement. The rooster had to be the standout. I walked around and around in the August dust. There was one rooster who stood tall above the rest, whose sheeny tail forked splendid purple in the afternoon sun, and who strutted. He fit the description in the book. After some hours of looking, I took that tall rooster and two matched pullets, and we put them into a cardboard box in the backseat of the '41 Chevy and drove to the fair.

The Arapahoe County fairgrounds were on a hill, spread over about a 25-acre lot. In the center, there was pink cotton candy, Cokes, hot dogs, a fine loudspeaker, and the rodeo and Catch-It-Calf arena for nighttime shows. The rodeo was the heart of the Fair for the old people. But for us, the future of America, the up-and-coming, would-be leaders in 4-H, it was the stock show and the competition that mattered. On the day before Fair, a hundred trailers started pulling up and backing into the barns. Cows were bawling; horses were kicking the sides of trailers; men, boys, and girls were racing around chasing whatever got loose or got into somewhere it was not supposed to be. Hardest to catch, and most dangerous, were escaped hogs. One night an ambulance came screaming into the fairgrounds because a young boy was gored by his own big hog. I think he was sleeping with his animal when it suddenly got tired of company. Sleeping with the stock was what a lot of people did, though. It was making sure a prized animal, the best a person had, stayed safe. This is what the young people told their folks, anyway. Then they got to lie down in the straw and whisper all night through the slats between the stalls. It was rumored, though I am sure I do not know, that now and again a future rancher and his female competition in the stall next door would get together to settle their differences peacefully. Which could help to explain why a lot of young people developed such a serious interest in the security of their stock.

Not me, though, not with my chickens. The pen was too small. Anyway, I would have had a tough time convincing anyone in my house that my chickens were good enough to be in some kind of danger.

There were different barns for sheep, pigs, calves, and horses. Just outside were concrete wash slabs where America's future leaders were hosing and washing everything from pigs to calves to some pretty unhappy sheep. Fortunately for me, we never did try to shampoo chickens, so I could just put my trio in the pen and watch all this commotion. There were also buildings filled with tables covered with pies and cakes and racks of fine, homemade dresses. Dresses, pies, and wheat seed were definitely out of my league. It is about all a person can do to learn chickens if he surely is going to make it in the real world. There were barns for fancy show birds, which were practically useless in real life, and for pumpkins and corn and wheat and hybrids which were, frankly, a little too useful for my taste. In the chicken barn there were fancy black roosters, trios of red Rhode Islands, White Rocks, funny-looking specialty birds, guineas and turkeys, and of course, rows of New Hampshires like mine.

By eleven or twelve at night on the day before Fair, the commotion began to settle down. Parents collected their broods and herded them home, unless they were kids who were going to sleep in the pens. Nobody would sleep that well, either in the pens or at home. Early in the morning, as soon as there was light, all the hoses and shampooing would begin again outside the barns, every head of stock getting one last soaping before midmorning, when the pens opened and out came the kids, one at a time, leading calves or sheep or horses all to different judging areas. The animals sparkled and glistened most unnaturally. The judges just stood there and glowered.

Well, there isn't any point in being coy about it. Not everybody wins. Smoky took seventh out of seven entries in her class at the Fair, and that was a pretty big blow. Erik led her around the ring, all shampooed to look like the shiniest dapple gray anyone had ever seen; but she was a plump sort of mare, and the judge told him to move her back one in the circle, and back one more, and gradually one by one, every horse entered was put ahead of him in the line. "Character building" is what my mother called it, as if it was good for him, even if it was hard. But that night we all treated Erik very nicely.

I went over to the chicken pens to watch the judging. Erik was the best stockman in the family, and his fate did not bode well. If he had had that bad luck, I was not very hopeful for my chickens. They were a pen of three, a group to be judged together. If one of them was good enough, that one would be judged against all the rest of the birds in the Fair, regardless of breed. Each pen had a tag on it with a secret number for the owner. The judge, who was a white-haired old man with a potbelly, came along the row of cages with a clipboard and a pencil. I stood back in among the pens about two aisles away, out of sight. The judge hesitated a little while looking over my threesome. He was interested but did not say anything to anyone. He moved on. No marks on the tag. He went up and down the aisles of pens. I hovered in the corner by the straw bales. I did not want to influence him by standing there like a little kid. I went across the fairgrounds to see Erik, who was doing all right, but he looked pretty sick. I came back. There was a new penciled circle on my tag. Inside the circle was the number one. I looked at it real hard. I went to find someone, *anyone,* to tell or ask. I went running for Erik, but then thought that would not be good, I might make him feel worse. I went looking for my mother. I went looking for someone who knew what the numbers in the circles meant. I found a friend from our 4-H club, an older person. I took him to my tag. He said that the number one meant that my three chickens had been ranked tops, best among all the trios of New Hampshires. I had first place and would get a blue ribbon. I tried to be very quiet. I tried not to be what my father would call "cocky." Cocky was not good in our family. Still, I went racing around wildly looking for my mother. I couldn't find her. I came back to the pens and there was another circle on my tag. The judging had continued. The new circle had a "GC" inside it. One of those fifty yellow chicks from my basement was now a GC. A lady walked by leading a little girl by the hand, looking at all the chickens in the cages. She said to the girl: "See, darling, 'GC' is for the Grand Champion. It's the rooster there." She turned to look at me. "Maybe it belongs to this young man here."

I stood gaping at her, dumb. Someone near me apparently was the owner and shower of the Grand Champion rooster of the whole Arapahoe County Fair. There wasn't anyone else around, though. I didn't want to be impolite, so I nodded, heart in my throat, hoping I would not be struck dead for claiming something that probably would not turn out to be true. I went on nodding for quite a while, not knowing what to say, until the little girl thought that nodding was the only thing I was able to do and lost interest in either me or the chickens. Finally the mother and girl left and I raced around the fairgrounds trying to find someone to tell.

I decided not to tell Erik, at least not for a while. But on the last night of the Fair, Erik caught a Catch-It-Calf. Suddenly, he had cattle. One cattle. He could plan his ranch. Smoky may not have been a show horse, but she had some speed and could surely herd cattle. So Erik had the makings, too. All was right with our world, after all.

12.

Smoky's Revenge

AFTER ERIK WON THE CATCH-IT-CALF, he raised the animal in the back corral and sent a letter once a month to the donating bank in Littleton. This letter was a report that the calf was gaining weight on schedule, etc., things that make a bank owner feel proud of America. Erik would not say, *Well, this month the fence was down and the calves were out as far as Dry Creek.* Or, *We lost them for three days.* Or, *It sure would be great if we had water out to the barn so we didn't have to carry slopping buckets every morning and afternoon from the house.* He included no details that showed a lack of control. Banks like control. The 4-H leader said that reports to banks require a little distance from what is really going on. "Too much reality," he said, "can darn near paralyze a bank." In the same way, Erik never reported that we found a nest with speckled pheasant eggs in the deep alfalfa or blue robin's eggs in a fork in a cottonwood branch. "Such things are nice," cautioned the 4-H man, "but not that interesting to city people who are mostly interested in the feel of money. For a bank president," he said, "you have to stick with things like a calf's weight, grain costs, expected date of slaughter, reports that show firmness. Banks like to hear about toughness and about time. How much time, how many pounds, how much ratio of gain to slop, things like that."

So, once a month, Erik thanked the local bank president, reporting that his calf was gaining weight. He avoided the temptation to become personally attached to his animal, which would not have been businesslike. Pretty soon he sold his fatted, golden calf for a 4-H-approved gain on investment, which was not too hard since he paid zero for it. Then he turned around and reinvested the proceeds in two or three more white-faces and we had a corral full. He bought three little ones for the price of the one he sold. "This is the way," my father said one night at dinner, "that great ranches are started. You could get to be another John Chisum. Maybe someday we'll have to do a cattle drive to Dodge City." My father never admitted to teasing. He wiggled his nose, though, which was a clue.

Frank got out his slide rule to figure out how long it would take three calves to turn into 5,000, with a rate of loss of one each year for every 600th Arapahoe County rattlesnake, assuming, that is, that there were, say, 7,500 rattlesnakes in the whole county and only one in 600 would actually bite one of our cows, minus the effects of blizzard depletion and natural abortions. "It'll take awhile," he pronounced conclusively, laying the slide rule beside the potatoes.

For me the only significance of all this palaver was more work. As much fence as we fixed, you would have thought it would stay fixed. But there were mornings that it did not stay fixed and the calves would be halfway to Kansas. I would be filling the water buckets in the kitchen sink to take out to the chickens or slopping through the mud, one bucket in each hand, and there would come this shout from the barn: "Calves are out!" That was the signal to drop everything and climb into the Chevy. My mother grabbed the keys and into the car we would go, driving around Arapahoe County looking for Erik's calves. Out past Curtis School, out where the wheat met the prairie, there they were, mingling with the antelope or magpies, enjoying the promise of American freedom.

Being youngest and smallest, I could not claim to know anything about a cow's thinking, like Erik or Frank, who would unload the car and plot the capture. My thing was to run. If the calves were east, and they were always east, I would run north, heading out through the plowed ground or the prairie sage far into what looked like the wrong direction. They, unsuspecting, would think I was headed back to Denver for lunch. Then, when I found cover or trees to the north, up under a line of cottonwoods or behind some willow brush, I swung east toward Kansas, or dropped behind the cover of long, rolling brown hills. Finally, when I was practically to Kansas City, I would pop up to the east side of the poor dumb beasts and run them home toward Erik and Frank, who waited by the car still plotting. This was their way of letting me help or letting me feel more like a man.

We had a neighbor by the name of Gene Cervi. His place was across Savage's wheat field out our kitchen window. Cervi had been in politics and was chairman of the Democratic Party of Colorado. My mother said that this is what happens to you when you run for office and lose. If you lose big enough, all your rivals think you are finished so they make you chairman. We would have liked Cervi even if he was not chairman because his family and ours were about fifty percent of all the Democrats in the whole of Arapahoe County. We had to stick together. As it happened, we lived side by side, about a third of a mile apart.

Gene Cervi was a little noisy. He used to say, with a twinkle, that he had been to dinner in all the great houses of Colorado once. "Never get invited back," he said.

"He's sort of a tub-thumper," my mother said.

Gene Cervi was dead-set earnest about life, loss, poor people, miners' tragedies, and all the things that rich people try to forget. But he was blustery like a prairie storm. "This day, of all days, rain will come!" he said. Real ranchers just said, "Rain coming." Farmers said, "This could be the day." Cervi said: "No question about it! Weather's changing! We will have a wet June, you can count on that, and hog futures will be down eight percent!" Cervi liked to be the first one to predict that things were going down. Down fit his prediction for a self-indulgent world.

"It's what makes him a good Democrat," said my mother, laughing.

Cervi lived in a modest converted chicken coop, low and flat to the ground. He roared when he talked about the rich, like a lion about to go on the hunt. He wrote about them in his own weekly newspaper, *Cervi's Journal*, which he founded to tell the world what wheat farmers think about banks. Over the years, the *Journal* became a must read for the business community in Denver. Everybody wanted to know what gossip Cervi was passing on about somebody else's financial affairs, which were usually "dismal."

Gene had a son named Mike whom, when he gave him a big red gelding, was about fifteen. "That's a pretty horse," my mother said one day over dishes. "Come look." We all gathered in the kitchen. Sure enough, across the back fence was a long-legged racer, pretty and sleek, a clean white slash on his red nose. "My, my," she said.

Not long after that, Mike Cervi took to riding up and down the canal by our place. He would ride up to the kitchen door and sit up there high in the air like the king of England, looking down at all the poor people streaming out of the house to see the big red. "Good-looking horse, Mike," said my mother, "*Beautiful* horse." My mother liked to make people feel good. She didn't feel the same need that my father did not to overdo, or to be a little cautious, so she just right out told people what she thought, at least when it was good.

"Yes, ma'am," said Mike. "We got this horse over to Burlington." Then he told us what the weather was like the day they got that horse and how they traded for some hay and a hundred bucks. He told how the wheat was tall down there, but not any taller than here, not really, and you could see two-headed calves down there to Burlington very easy, if you knew where to look. We all just stood there, goggle-eyed.

"Want to see him run?" Everybody on the ground nodded. So Mike took the red horse up on the ditch road, never stopped talking, and took off in a cloud of thunder, words trailing behind him like stones bouncing in the dust. I felt a little sad to see that horse because I knew we would never own an animal like that. Too pretty. Our family believed in things that were useful. Sleek and useful are about as apt to go together as a worm in soup.

Erik said, "More show than anything, really."

Every now and then, Mike's red gelding got out, like our calves. He'd get through the fence and disappear out on the prairie. *Neighbors are for helping,* said Erik, so when Mike came over and told us that Red was out, we would bridle up Chita and Captain and spread out over the draws and through the cottonwoods. When we found him, which we did regularly, Gene Cervi might even invite us into his chicken house for a piece of pie or a Coke, but we never accepted that because there was always fence to fix or something to do at home. We didn't know enough to sit down and talk to the great man who had all those connections and was famous.

Cervi did say, though, before we left, that he thought we would turn out all right in life, being boys that brought home other people's horses. And he would say that around town, too, and we heard about it, so we probably got something better than pie. It was nice like that, having neighbors who thought about how other neighbors' kids would turn out.

Cervi would talk to anyone. My father said that he supposed that self-assurance was a good thing but it definitely had to be kept in hand. *If you're good,* he said, *that's fine, but you needn't talk about it.* So even though we chased each other's stock and were neighbors, our families had that little difference in style.

Now it happened that one year at County Fair there were horse races. Smoky, as everybody knew, was round, but she was pretty fast. "She can move," Erik said one day, thinking about the Fair.

"Maybe a little fat," said Mike Cervi, who that day was sitting up on the big red, trying to help us be realistic.

"Well, chunky, shall we say," said my mother.

Chita was Frank's horse, and I rode her quite a lot when Frank was busy getting ready to go to college to be a significant engineer. So Erik and I decided to enter Smoky and Chita in the horse race at the County Fair, 4-H kids only. At the same time, Mike Cervi entered his big red gelding. Smoky was fast, and Chita was good around the corners, but the Cervi gelding was a horse. It didn't look so good for the county's leading family of modest nontalkers.

A few days before the race, the horses were housed in the barns at the fairgrounds. There were all the usual stock shows and the ferris wheels and the midway, where the fat lady was, and the shooting galleries. There were bump-o-cars where boys who were noticing girls for the first time could smash into them so as to show their interest and affection. I did that once and the pretty little blonde in the car that I had hit screamed and started to cry. I got the impression that I had failed, somehow.

There was cotton candy and the merry-go-round and music blaring: all that excitement, which was for kids, really, and not for real stockmen. As it turned out, the horse barns were located away from all that music and clanging of bells and shouting. Horses spook easy, and spooked horses have a mind of their own. So the horse barns were close beside the running track to make it easier to exercise them and to keep them away from the commotion over on the midway. In fact, the barns were cheek by jowl with the last turn on the track where the horses would come charging around, hell-bent for the finish. Every day we rode out from the barns onto the track through a little gate that opened right there.

A person could hear me talking. "This is it, horse. This is where we are going to fly. Get ready, horse, get ready." *Pat, pat.* Sometimes you just have to pat a horse on the neck to let her know you're up there. Out through the little gate. *Trot, trot* around the track. "Okay, now, run . . . Fly, horse, fly . . . good horse, good." Back through the gate, into the barn. "Tomorrow, horse, tomorrow. Be ready." *Pat, pat.* We never spoke a horse's name. Things were too tense to get sentimental.

Tomorrow comes and there are only seven entries. Most of them look a little more like running horses than either Smoky or Chita. Anyway, we are going to make a try for it. At this point I am not having many illusions about Chita. She is a pretty little black with a white streak down her nose. Pretty, and sometimes skittish and ornery. She is fast, though. But still, when we race down the canal, Erik always beats me. He is a better rider, has more courage. I am trying, at full run, so hard to hang on that I probably pull back some. Erik has better balance. Smoky is probably a little faster, too. We will be bareback. It can get pretty hairy at full speed. I am hoping, above all, to hang on. We ride out in front of the stadium and slowly trot around to the far side of the track. *Trot, trot.* Very tense. Some older person tells us to bunch up and raises a pistol into the air. We will go around one half of the track to race past the bleachers where the family is. That will be it. These are not long-range horses. The fastest we have ever gone before is to run from a skunk when its tail went up.

The gun pops and we are off. I can see Smoky quickly out in front of me. The big Cervi gelding is out there too. Smoky is second to the big red. I can't see much but the rising and falling of horse haunches in front of me, and I hear the pounding thunder of other horses beside and behind me. Mike is pulling away, I can tell that. Smoky and Erik are holding in second. We pound around the first turn and are still pretty much bunched together, except that Mike is getting a good lead. Then there are a lot of horse rear ends swarming around me. Now we are cooking. There is something that just plain gets into an ordinary horse, even a horse like Chita, when she starts to fly between two or three other animals running alongside.

This is where the horse is full-out gone. She is not domestic, or a farm horse, or trained. She becomes a wild thing, thundering along the track like an energy from the volcanic earth, sinuous, gathering in the shoulders and stretching out for turf, undulating, gathering again, pounding madly forward. We have entered a horse zone. A human child clings to the mane and is privileged, for a moment, to be one with the stallions, flying as stallions have flown over the prairies and steppes since before time. The twelve year-old wraps knees around jackhammer shoulders. There is mud flying from the hooves and dust in his eyes, there is rocking and swaying when we come into the turn, the bulging shoulders of a challenging horse beside us, the rippling great muscles pushing against my legs, and through all this there is screaming in the stands.

Erik and Mike and I are out there just flying, holding on. Erik and I are bareback to save precious weight. We are bareback because we are proud boys from the country showing off and because it is second nature to ride skin and bones next to skin and bones, body to body, soul to soul with the horses we have fed and watered for years. Mike is bareback too, and his red gelding is pulling away, stride by stride. Three kids, now, holding on with their legs for dear life and one hand along the neck, streaming into the final turn. Mike has the lead. It looks as if there will be no victory for shy people this day.

Then it happens. Suddenly Mike is gone. He is just gone. He just disappears. From my vantage, I am holding on, my head lying along the horse's neck; I have never flown so fast in all my life—and then there is a kind of rusty blur between Chita's ears as the big red gelding suddenly veers, streaking across the track toward the outside rail. Mike can't hold him. The horse knows where to go, like every other day, and out he goes, hell-bent for the barn. The gate is closed. Doesn't matter. The big red heads through wood, wire, and rails full-out at thirty miles per hour, like an elephant in heat.

I hear the crash. I don't know much because I am leaning my head along Chita's neck, breathing fire and happiness for being alive, and all of a sudden the Cervi gelding is gone from my world. I'm maybe second, maybe third; it doesn't matter because suddenly Smoky is in the lead. Erik and his dapple gray thunder across, win the race for all the shy people, all the fat horses, and all the odds-against underdogs in the world.

While we were still milling around on the track, someone in the bleachers turned to my mother and nodded toward the winning gray mare. "Fast, ain't she, for a damn plow horse."

"Gosh," answered my mother who was more or less speechless, "what a world."

Erik and Smoky won the blue ribbon for best and most memorable unexpected triumph in life and Mike won the drama contest, which was about right for both families, everything considered. Mike, who had been shot like a rocket off the track through the wood gate and into the barns, was okay. He was just a little sheepish when we finally found him wandering around the midway holding blankly onto some pink cotton candy, kind of wobbly, grinning weakly, set back but not down. "Damn," he smiled thinly. Just that once there was not another word in him.

13.

The Plow Horse Tries to Plow

THERE WAS A STRANGE MAN called Sam who drove around the dirt roads of the county in his horse and buggy, swearing and cursing at small boys playing in the fields. We might be racing wood chips down the feeder ditch, or chasing a lost calf, or standing out in the middle of the alfalfa haying, sweating in the hot summer sun. Along would come Sam in his buggy, cracking his whip, shouting obscenities, song, or the news about Communists, usually all in the same sentence. Sam was out of his head. He was not so lucky, probably, as all the rest of us who had hay fields and stock and friends. He seemed to have a good relationship with his horse, and he never caused me any grief except to scare me off the road. He was loud, though, and everybody gave him a wide berth. Everybody knew Sam.

"Hi, Sam!" my friend Darryl yelled whenever Sam came trotting around the bend, sitting up there in his buggy seat, flailing his whip in the wind. Sam would rattle off some very pointed but absolutely unintelligible reply that Darryl and I pretended to understand, but frankly I never got the gist of it.

Sam rode around the county roads for several years, waving his whip in the air, shouting at the cattle, or trees, or boys. He had black whiskers and a dirty face. He had a black horse and everything about him was smudged or black except for one shiny, red stripe that ran down both sides of his buggy, kind of pretty, really, just below the seat. Month after month, he trotted up and down the roads through wheat country.

"You know what I think?" said Darryl one day. "I think that old loon was talking about that red stripe!" I could not tell and I didn't think much about it. Maybe so, maybe not; it was not my affair and I was a little afraid of Sam.

There were not many people around who still drove buggies. The idea of it caught Erik's imagination. Erik could ride. He could win a horse race, he had shown that. He could fix fence and stack hay. He could do almost anything. But he had never tried hitching up a buggy. He thought about that for some months.

Then, as if by magic, that year at Christmas when we came into the living room singing the usual carols, there out the front window on the lawn was a buggy, big wooden wheels high in the grass. On the floor under the tree were all sorts of pieces of leather harness. "My, my," my mother said, mystically, "Santa has done it again."

When the snow melted and spring came, Erik decided it was time to hook up the buggy. He chose Captain as the pulling horse, because Captain was the biggest.

"This will be interesting," said my mother.

"Well, Smoky's too fat for the harness," said Erik. "And Chita's too small and spooks easy. Chita will spook at a fly."

"She's not that bad," said Frank, because Chita was his horse.

"Eat your spinach, both of you," said my mother.

Captain was a riding horse and all his life had never even been on the same side of the fence with a buggy, much less pulled one. Still, when it came to doing new things that had never been tried before, Erik was not a man to be put off by civilized caution. I could have helped here with a little common sense. Erik was older than I, though, and by definition he knew everything I did, plus a good deal extra. I ate my spinach without advising him.

So, come April, he, Frank, and Don picked a good quiet Saturday and Erik went out and put a rope around Captain's neck. Erik brought the big gangly horse around to the area near the asparagus patch that was out of the corral, away from the other horses, so if there was any trouble, it wouldn't spook the other two. Horse spookiness is infectious. Chita and Smoky might go straight through the fence where they could get cut up and tear out posts and mess up a whole lot of things, including our good moods. The asparagus area, on the other hand, was open to the road—that is, if they could ever get Captain headed away from the barn and over in that direction. Since Christmas, Erik had been studying all the pieces of leather harness and thought he knew what went where. He put the heavy collar around Captain's neck, and the big red horse shivered and shook. "Okay," said Erik, "that's step one."

I stood back about fifteen feet with plenty of room to keep on going. I would have settled for the neck collar or just a little more and come back to try the rest of that fancy harness some other day. *No rush, really,* I thought. But Erik said, "Okay, that's step one."

"Okay," Frank said.

Frank didn't look any better than I felt. He stood in front of Captain's nose, holding on to the headstall. Erik started to put on the rest of the leather contraption, one piece at a time. The straps looped all around and over the poor beast like a leather cobweb. Finally came the last strap, which was to go snug up under Captain's tail.

"Easy," said Frank.

"You don't have to tell me," said Erik. Captain was beginning to take exception to this whole procedure. The strap went under his tail. He shimmied and pranced and lifted his hind end about six inches off the ground. I moved back another ten feet where I could get a good head start if the whole operation suddenly went toward Kansas. "Whoa!" said Frank, holding Captain's 1,000-pound red hulk to his own 120-pound, clean white chest.

"Yeah, whoa," said Erik, grinning just a little, standing back, looking over his horse bedecked with every kind of strap and harness known to man. Erik was not one to lose heart just because of terror, so he rolled the buggy up and attached all the lines. Then he stepped back again to look the whole thing over one more time. He started to gather up the reins and head for the step up. At this point, Captain had had all he needed. Erik put his foot on the step, Captain heard the buggy springs squeak behind him, and he jumped forward. The buggy lurched to follow and the horse leapt again to get out of the way. The buggy bolted right behind him. Erik never made it aboard. Captain left him running along in the dust, grabbing for reins or harness or whatever, and then got completely away. The horse plunged down the road past our house, careened around the mailbox at the front road, headed for another county, headed for kingdom come. We stood in a silent little cluster and watched him charge down the hill. Pretty soon, the buggy started coming apart one piece at a time and, with every piece that flew off, Captain spooked worse and ran faster. Erik scraped the buggy off some cottonwoods down by Darryl's place. That was the end of one quiet Saturday afternoon, and after that we did not do that fool thing ever again, so far as I remember.

"What was the point of that?" Erik asked at dinner, feeling pretty glum, angry at himself.

Nobody knew the point.

"Well, you had to try it," said my mother.

"It might have worked with Chita," offered Frank.

"Nooo, it would not have worked with Chita," said Erik, hanging his head.

"Maybe it would have worked if you had a red stripe down the side of the buggy," said my father. He wriggled his nose.

"I doubt it," said Erik.

"Maybe," said Frank, "I could have held him."

"No, you did the best you could," said Erik.

"Well, Sam's better at some things than the rest of us," said Don, being serious. "I guess there's a lesson in that."

"What lesson?" said Erik.

"Tolerance, maybe," said Don.

"Could be," said Erik. "Could be."

After the great buggy crash, we began to see differently. We did not laugh at Crazy Sam because he was tetched. He was a miracle worker with a buggy. He could turn on a quarter, he could hold his buggy horse in a sustained trot, he could take her to a gallop full-out along the Highline ditch road, and he always kept the red stripe so you could see it, shiny and bright. *He can do something,* said my father appreciatively, *that we will not ever be able to do.*

Erik, however, was not a man for standing around counting posies or someone else's red decorations. I found him out in the corral one day standing there, looking at Smoky with an evil eye. "The fatter, the better to plow," he said. That was all the consideration it took, and after that Erik began looking for a plow. "This could be useful," he told Don, "for plowing the front so you could someday plant grass."

There was about a half-acre area in front of the house that was full of weeds and my mother's seedling trees. There was a lingering threat forever hanging in the air that small boys were going to have to spade up that whole big area before it could be seeded in grass. Erik was thinking about an easier way. "It could be Smoky could pull," he said, looking over the gray mare.

So one day it was Smoky's turn. Same thing as Captain. Smoky was out there in front of the house, only instead of being nervous about the harness, she took it just fine. Erik got the whole harness wrapped around the horse and stepped back and looked at her and the hand plow in the ground just behind her. Smoky stood there placid, as if she was born to plow. A plow connects to the harness by a thing called a "singletree." This is a wooden pole that hooks up between the plow and the harness at three places and hangs lengthwise across the back of the horse. Somewhere Erik had found the plow and the singletree, but none of it was new. In fact, the old singletree was gray with age, the plow was rusty, the wood handles were grooved from weathering. "Rust won't matter," Erik said, "to the ground."

Everything was ready to go. Smoky did not need nearly the control that Captain had needed, and there was no danger that the plow would sing and squeak as the buggy did. "Can't run the plow around the corners like that buggy," Erik said. He stepped behind the plow and flipped the reins along the horse's back. "Let's go," he said with a nervous grin. Smoky began to pull. The plow dug in. Smoky leaned in and pulled harder. The plow wedged in the clay soil and went deeper. The leather lines stretched tighter.

Suddenly, the singletree snapped. It broke with a sound like a cannon shot. The noise exploded over Smoky and sent her leaping into the air as if someone had jammed her in the soft behind with a hot poker. The plow twisted loose from the earth and wrenched out of Erik's hands, and off she went. This time the wreck occurred over on Savage's fence. The plow, Smoky, and fence were twisted into some kind of modern sculpture. Smoky stood there shivering and shaking until Erik caught up to free her.

"There should be something to learn from this," said my mother later at dinner, laughing.

"Yeah," said Erik, glum again. "But what?"

Nobody knew what.

So my mother said, "Well, are you going to try it again?"

"If we keep losing horses down the road, we are going to have to dig the lawn by hand anyway, "Frank said.

"Well, the singletree's broken," Erik said, giving in for the moment to the end of his plowing career. He went back to being a cowboy and Smoky went back to being a retired racehorse, and the big lawn was dug by hand. "Manual labor is a sign of solidarity with the working class, don't you know?" said my mother, probably because she did not have to dig. But the real reason Erik had to give up all this extracurricular horsemanship was that he was running out of equipment that was still in one piece. We didn't have anything more to try, or he would have tried it.

14.

The Last Log Barn

BY NOW WE HAD A CORRAL FENCE, three horses, a chicken coop, ducks and chickens, calves, and for a while, a pig. We even had turkeys. But turkeys are so dumb nobody really knows what to do with them. They eat more or less the same as chickens, so I had to feed them, but I did not adopt them as part of my official calling. I never said I was a turkey farmer. It is hard enough to be an expert on chickens. It is not a prestige thing to be connected with something even dumber than chickens. Chickens are at least ten percent smarter than turkeys.

I think it was my mother who wanted something bigger and more dramatic. She said that turkeys could be stately and elegant, that this USA was founded on turkeys, and Samuel Sewall probably even ate turkeys. She used the Sewall argument, I knew, when she had a weak case, because it is hard to justify anything so dumb. *But,* she said practically, *turkeys might be quite tasty.*

So we started out with a dozen little turkey chicks. But the chicks were out one day and saw the smooth surface of the little irrigation feeder ditch and tried to walk across. Which they could not do, of course, so they drowned. It wasn't long before we had only a few left.

"Walking on water could be a valuable contribution to science if you could make it work," said my father. My mother was sorry. She had in mind growing them at least until Thanksgiving. Maybe the turkeys thought it was a losing proposition either way.

That autumn the two or three turkeys we had left after the water-walking experiment began pecking on the Thanksgiving wreath on the front door of the house. They hammered so hard on the wreath that the door opened. When we came home for dinner one November night, we found two turkeys roosting on the back of the couch in the living room. Turkeys don't respond to directions very well. Not like sheep, where you can just get behind and push them the way you want. So we had a time persuading the turkeys to wake up and head for the front door rather than to the dining room or the bedrooms. "Whoosh! Whoosh! Whoosh!" screamed my mother. When they were gone, feathers were everywhere and the couch did not look too good.

My mother had made a fantastic wreath of fruits and dried grains, which was now drooping in ruins from our front door. "They were just pecking to get at the corn and fruit you put up there," said my father, laughing, sweeping up red and orange corn bits.

"Not likely," said my mother, her face shining. "This is a political protest. This is how the mine workers got started, sitting in someone's living room!"

"Maybe," said Don, bending his face up to look at her with a crinkly shy smile. "Maybe that's true." His face was full of affection and wonder at the woman he had got.

That Christmas, because I had demonstrated that I could take care of my chickens, Don was sitting on the floor with a woolly lamb in his arms, and I went into the sheep business. We were getting to be quite an outfit. We also had two dogs and two cats, but they don't count as anything real, because they were just about like people. In our house neither the dogs nor cats were real or important, because to be real a thing has to be mostly work.

We named the cats Black Cat and Kitty. "You will get no points for imagination on those names, boys," said my mother, who did not care much about cats. But we said, *Why give a cat a personal name, anyway, since it will never come when it is called? Cats are good to keep mice out of the kitchen*, she agreed, in the same tone of voice she used for bats and garter snakes. There was no way a cat could be a real-life friend, like children or horses, because you could as well train a chicken or a duck as a cat.

My dog Stormy was born one night in the basement while I scrunched on the floor beside the box. He was the firstborn in a litter of about eight. Since he was the first, and I was there, he was the one I chose to keep. My mother said his breed was Heinz 57, which meant he was like Heinz soups, as mixed as noodles and peas. Stormy was mixed black and white; he was going to be long-haired with a flowing tail. I wanted him to be mine the moment his mother started licking him and I could see how pretty he was. I raised him from as soon as he was weaned, and after that he got to know the trails through the buckbrush along the canal just as well as I did. As soon as he could run, we went everywhere together. He had English setter blood as one of his fifty-seven varieties, so he liked to quarter the fields for pheasants. We were a team, ranging the fields and bushes along under the cottonwoods, looking for excitement.

We now had one or two of about everything, from dogs to horses to sheep, a temporary pig, and a passel of chickens. But there was no place for the stock to get in out of the blowing snow in winter. Lambs are born in the spring, February mostly, when the temperature can get well below zero, cold enough to finish off any newborn thing. So my father, who worked professionally as an engineer, decided to build a barn.

"Good," he said one day when we were out in the corral at the proposed location. I was holding tight on a survey string. He was pulling on the other end, and we were measuring the length of the west wall of the new barn.

He said "good," but I knew it was not so good because when he pulled the steel tape tight to measure the length of the wall, he pulled so hard that I could not hold my end. It was off by at least two inches. I was afraid to tell him, since I was supposed to hold the tape directly over a nail in the dirt. When he started to lean with all his 175 pounds backward on the tape, I strained and strained, but my fingers could not hold it. I knew how important it was to him to be exact, and I was afraid to say that the tape had been off a little without making it seem like it was his fault for pulling too hard. So I was in a fix I did not know how to get out of. All this made me feel stupid, but I just hoped that in the long course of my life, somehow it would all work out and the barn would be a good two inches shorter or longer, either way. It didn't feel good, though, knowing that I couldn't really do a man's job.

He staked out the dimensions of the new barn, with or without my two inches, and then hitched the old two-wheel trailer to the back of the '41 Chevy and drove along to the Big Bend of the canal. Down in there under the cottonwoods, he could get the trailer off the wheel track close to the bottom of the canal where there was plenty of good sand for mixing with concrete. We had to stand down in the ditch and shovel about four feet back up to the trailer. I did a little better shoveling sand than I did holding the tape. I had seen other kids who were even bigger than me throw sand in wide arcs that drifted and scattered and never made a clean pile in the bed of the trailer. Those kids did not quite have the makings. They could be leftover people, more than likely stuck in cities.

So I learned to twist the shovel in my wrists just at the moment when the sand leaves the spade so that it will sail bunched in a high arc and no part flies in the wind or misses the bed of the trailer. *When a man does it just right,* said my father, *the whole shovelful goes* thump *in the corner right where you want to put it.* Sure enough, one day, thump, went my sand. One shovelful after the next. *Thump. Thump. Yes,* he said. *Not many boys as small as you can do that.* At that time I was almost as long as the shovel handle, which seemed big enough to me. But I liked the compliment and ever after that I never minded when my father was trying to round up someone to go shovel sand. *Yeah,* I always said, *I've got time.*

After the foundations were poured, on Saturdays from June to August, we were all rousted out of bed before daylight and piled into the Chevy. Don hitched up the same trailer we had used for sand, but now we headed for Squaw Peak, thirteen thousand feet above sea level. First thing to do when we got there was gather wood for a cooking fire. Then my mother cooked a breakfast of eggs and bacon, pancakes and syrup. Her campfire pancakes didn't hold together that well, so I ate a lot of pancake crumbs, grease, syrup, crumbling bits of dough, butter and smoke, right out of the black frying pan. This was, by any reckoning, the best part of any Saturday.

I was too small to use an axe, so my job was to squat by the fire, eat leftover pancakes, run for more wood, or later, drag big logs down the mountain after my father had cut them. My older brothers did not have time to eat so much. They scouted for the best spars to cut, ranging off through the pine forest, trying to find dead trees about the right size for a true beam, a door-jamb, or a wall. Don would go up to a spar and size it up as if he was looking over a thin-print engineering diagram. *Cut here, I should think,* he would mumble to himself, judging where to chop to get the tree to fall without hanging up in the branches of other pines. He handled an axe like it was the natural extension of his arm. "Like the early days in Oregon," he said, and yelled "TIMMBERR!" even though the only people for miles around were me and Erik and Frank and we were standing right there. So we all three jumped back about ten feet and watched the big trees fall. Erik and Frank stripped the limbs with small axes, and then I grabbed hold of the thin end and dragged the logs downhill.

Past the campfire, beside the road, we loaded the logs into the trailer and tied a red flag to the longest pole. When the loading was done, we slowly headed home. Once the trailer was full, it had to be downhill only or burn out the Chevy's clutch. The only place we ever found that went down all the way was Squaw Mountain, which is why we always went there for logs.

Since it was Saturday, not really a workday, and there was nothing to do but ride and wait, Don turned on the car radio and we listened to programs from back east, or mysteries or news. He would never listen to popular music. For him, popular music was like fingernails on a blackboard. "Not really very serious," said Frank. Which was okay with me. I had heard enough to know those love songs were mostly about people who were carrying on. I had been warned enough about carrying on not to want to get sweet-talked into that. So we listened to football games, which we all agreed were more constructive.

It would be three or four in the afternoon when we finally pulled into the corral. It didn't take long to drag the logs off the trailer and stack them. Captain and Chita came over and sniffed. The lambs and ewes came out and tried to butt heads with Stormy, who was nipping at their heels, trying to round them up like pheasants. Chickens clucked and calves bawled. One by one, Don began to select logs to lay on his concrete foundation. Each one had to be sawed into an exact size, then the knobs had to be chopped off and the top and bottom smoothed to level. Finally, each end had to be notched. This went on for most of June. I didn't say anything about the two inches I had lost when we were doing the measurements, but it still worried me some.

My favorite tool was the adz, partly because it was the most dangerous. "Careful," Don said one day, because an adz has a flat, wide blade that swings directly toward a man's legs. "Careful. An adz can take a small boy's ankle in a single swing." It was the adz that made a rough log smooth, top and bottom, and it was used to cut notches in the ends where the logs would join. It was what prepared the wood for the careful work of the chisel that he would do. There was another reason I wanted to use it; if I did the notching, I would be getting my work right up next to his; the little kid could be useful for the man, and I wanted that.

"Can I try it?" I asked.

"Very careful," he said, barely taking his eyes from the log he was notching.

Raising chickens was one thing. Any small boy could walk around and watch the chickens cluck, or could collect eggs and close the door of the coop at night. Skunks were said to be a danger, and I had kept my chickens from skunks. But really no one ever saw a skunk eat a chicken, and the danger was sort of a myth to make little kids feel good, as if they had protected something. Feeding and watering was now normal, too, in the course of my day. I could do that as well as anyone. Building a barn was different. Men who built barns worked all day from morning to night and never got tired. They lifted logs and were broad in the shoulders. I thought that building something with my brothers and father was the last thing I needed to show I was getting older. Somewhere, too, maybe I could get that two inches back that I had lost on the west side, and maybe the adz would give me the chance.

"Careful," he said.

What with all the commotion of Stormy chasing the sheep, hens clucking, and horses shuffling among us, there was bound to be some problem. It happened one day that the big red horse, Captain, was sniffing in the midst of the tools and the chopping. He thought it was his corral, and it was definitely not smart for me to be swinging a sharp adz with that big animal standing too close. "Don't do it," said Don. "Get that big, red lummox out of there." He stared at the horse nibbling on my shoulder. "Craig, you get distracted and it's a sure way to take a leg off."

On most days, as a matter of habit, we just walked past Captain, said "Shoo!" and waved an arm. He would lift his nozzle from whatever can of nails he was about to turn over and step away, but only a foot or two. Then he would drift back and nose around the back end of Frank or Erik, who might be bent over hammering or pounding logs. The horse could nibble Levi's and just barely catch enough skin underneath to make a hammering man leap up in the air.

"Beat it!" said Frank.

"You trying to keep your pants on?" asked my father, chuckling.

"Yes!" said Frank. "He's a pest! I like my pants on!"

Captain drifted off to go chew on a wooden hammer he found lying on the ground. "Cut it out!" said Erik, who had left the hammer just long enough to go and steady the other end of Frank's log. "Cut it out! Drop that thing!" He got off Frank's log and went after the horse, which moved back toward Frank's vulnerable rear end. "Shoo!" said Frank.

Don had stopped work and was standing up full, laughing, while the horse sauntered over toward the chicken shed.

About that time, my mother, walking out of the house with lunch in her arms, headed for the chicken shed where she could sit down to pass out soup and sandwiches. She fixed her eye on the same flat place that Captain had decided was the only sheltered area a horse could have to himself.

"Shush!" she said, kicking a foot in the air, like she was threatening Kitty or Black Cat out of the kitchen. "Shush!" But Captain was not a cat.

The horse was turned away, rear end toward her, and could not go the direction he was being shushed because it was a dead end into the chicken shed. So he laid his ears back and lifted his hind end and kicked her.

It cost her two broken ribs and sent her to bed. She looked pale and lay there trying to decide whether it was more painful to breathe or not to breathe. I never saw her pale before. I never saw her sick before. She lay awfully still, trying to breathe only the smallest little bit to stay alive.

I could use an adz now, all right, but I was not so grown up I knew how to make soup. Frank and Erik were only a little better. I guess Don knew how to open a can, but he was not swift. That night we stood and looked at her under the pale sheets, her white face drawn. "You definitely are out of your element, boys," she grinned weakly when we were huddled by the bed and she heard of our efforts in the kitchen. "Well, hold on. I'm all right. I'll be there in the morning." We didn't know what to think. We had never seen her down. Women didn't get sick as far as we knew. We didn't know if they stayed sick, either, but she sure didn't look like she should be walking around.

"Darn horse," said Erik, who could almost swear because this was really serious, and could swear at this horse because it was his. None of the rest of us said anything about the horse because it was not our place. "Sorry," said Erik, standing there looking down at her pale face. "Really sorry."

"These things happen," she said.

"There's pea soup, and we could do hamburgers, I think," said Erik.

"Anything," she said, "that is soft. Soup. Not hamburgers." Her eyes crinkled a little through the pain. "Just don't make me laugh."

She couldn't bear to lie still. The doctor said she ought to stay in bed for a week. We puttered around outdoors in the corral for a couple of days doing all the same things on the barn, but we were weaker than usual because nobody in that house except her could cook. Since she couldn't get out of bed we were eating soup, Cheerios, and Shredded Wheat. Every now and then one of us would make an excuse to stop hammering or using the adz and go in and check on her. She looked so pale you could not tell where the sheet ended and her chin began. We held water for her so she would not have to move her arms, but she did not like that much. I mean, she liked the water and she liked not moving her arms, but being helped for every little thing went against the grain. Maybe this was not the lifetime for her to get used to that. "Oh, heavens!" she said, "I can drink!"

After two days, that was the end of it. She said, "My, my, you boys look peaked. Cereal and sugar are not enough to build a barn on!" Next morning she was back on her feet, puttering around in the kitchen. We came in from doing chores and there she was. "You get on back to the barn," she said. "Summer will be over soon." She didn't say it very loud because she was saving her breath and still didn't like the idea of breathing all that much.

"It looks like it still hurts," said Frank.

"Oh, no!" she said, even though her lips were drawn tight. "It is just one of those things." But her face stayed pale for at least a week, and we tried to clean our feet at the back door and clean our dishes after dinner and do all sorts of unnatural but kind things.

After I tried my hand at the adz, Don chiseled smooth joints for clean fittings, then we raised the walls, one log at a time, and braced and double-braced the crossbeams. Summer and winter, all through one year and the next, the logs kept on going up. When the height got to be too much, Don would lift and guide the poles upward, sometimes with me pushing on an end or helping to steady the long sway of a twenty-foot spar, while Erik and Frank sat balanced astride the top high beam, pulling and inching each new log into place.

"Easy there, easy, it's sneaking over on the left!" Don watched my brothers from below as they tried to pull up the weight of a log without being levered off their perches. When they had the beam in place, each began pounding through the carefully chiseled notch that had been prepared down below. They were hammering large, twenty-penny spikes. When a nail that big is driven through a pine log, it makes a clean, solid ring, like an anvil. It sounds good and feels forever.

"Well, I don't know about you," said Don, looking up at the boys pounding high atop the rising walls, "but I think it had better be right the first time. I don't think we're ever going to take those spikes out!"

When the space was enclosed, walls on four sides, it was time to lay the great roof beams, which were the longest and strongest of all that we had worked with. But by now we were old hands. The roof was braced and double-braced again. Don was a man for double-bracing.

"Can you lift that pole end up to me?" He was perched, one day, high on the main crossbeam and the other boys were somehow not around. We were into our second year and hurrying to beat October snowfall. I did what he asked, leaning toward a long, twenty-foot log, hoisting it to my shoulder, then jacking it forward a foot at a time until the long end edged up high enough for him to reach it.

"Is it my imagination, or are you getting stronger?" He looked down at me where I was steadying the heavy end.

A man could wait a long time for words like that. But there was no sense in replying. I held the heavy end of the log. "Ready," I said, "when you are," and at his nod, I heaved the pole up to where he could get a full hold and lever it into position.

That October, the barn was finished.

On a cold February morning, my first lambs were born in a well-chinked, dry corner. "Well, that's fine," he said. In spring the chickens moved in, and then the ducks.

"All right," he said one day out in the hot fields of sun-drenched summer, as I scrambled on top of the alfalfa stack and trampled hay through the morning and afternoon, hour by hour. The stack was building on a big, movable wagon we called a "rick." This was hay to be stored for the horses, calves, and sheep, stacked in and near the new barn. Barn, hay, fence, and livestock; we had the makings of a spread. Hay leaves stuck to my sweaty back and stomach, and to his, and all through our hair. All day long at the top of the stack I bounced over to each new pitchfork that swept up toward me from the men in the field. As was the custom, neighbors were helping us, just as we sometimes helped them, and I wanted to do it right because strangers were watching. I jumped up and down to wedge the stack into a woven, stable mesh, or rearranged it with my own fork so that it would wall out straight on the sides and not slope in, or so that pieces would not slide out on the drive home. The faster the hay came up, the faster my pitchfork swept the alfalfa this way and that. Smooth, smoother, tamped down tight for the ride back to the barn. By noon, my legs ached and bent or nearly buckled beneath me, but I tried not to pay any attention.

That afternoon I was like a man possessed; I leapt from corner to corner of the rick, catching each new pitchfork full of hay like it was gold, sorting it out, laying it smooth, looking for more. The day wore on and my legs held up. I was not as long as the pitchfork, but I knew how to use one.

"All right," Don said at the end of the day. The July sun was drifting down over Mount Evans in the west and I slid down the side of my haystack. He had been waiting for me. He went to the cab of the Chevy and got my shirt and handed it to me. We walked home together across the cut field, a pitchfork on his shoulder, another on mine. Then we walked along without a word, just the two of us, through the stubble of cut alfalfa toward the old bridge that crossed the irrigation canal and that was home to the blue-tailed swallows. We walked along, he and I alone, under the shimmering cottonwoods, working buddies, two people who pitch hay all day and don't get tired because they are nearly too strong to ever be tired.

"All right, rascal," he said as we stored the pitchforks in the corner of the new barn.

We stood in a tight corner. He knew every log and had chiseled and shaped them all, one at a time. He didn't know, I realized with a sinking feeling, about the time when I had missed the measurement for the west wall. I screwed up my courage. *This would be a good time,* I thought.

"You know," I said, "one time, at the beginning when we were measuring for this barn, you told me to hold the tape, but I could not do it. I lost at least two inches here on the west side. I have been worried about that ever since. Did you notice that? I mean, I may have messed it up."

He turned to look at me. We were in the shadow of pine logs tightly notched and hewed to lie close together. Here and there, rays of the setting sun peeked through a hole or crack between the beams.

"Now, that can be a problem sometimes," he said, sucking in a deep breath. I could feel my grown-up status about to drain out the soles of my feet.

"I suppose it was hard for you to hold the tape?"

I nodded, but did not speak.

"I should have thought of that," he said.

I was looking at my boots in the dirt floor. I shuffled my feet and dust rose.

He said: "We try as hard as we can, I think, and still some sun comes through the cracks. It does that for all of us." I looked up. His face was caught in a ray of light that squeezed through the logs from where the sun was setting in the west over Mount Evans. He was looking at a coil of dust motes that fell between us, shimmering and dancing in the last beams of sunlight. "Don't worry. I imagine we got your two inches back. Anyway, it's kind of pretty this way, don't you think?" I looked at the golden dust between us and wanted to cry like a kid.

He moved toward me to rub my hair. I looked up. He had stopped where the glow surrounded his face and a sunbeam seemed to fall directly into the pupils of his eyes so that they glowed amber and gold. Then I saw that his eyes were moist, too. "Proud of you," he whispered. "Proud of you all. We just do the best we can."

Chicks were hatched and lambs were born in that barn. Hay was stacked there, and grain was stored in the old casket case we got from our friend the mortuary man. We never thought too much about where the casket came from. We never thought about death. Over the years, mostly the log barn was a place where things were born. Lambs, ducks, and small boys on their way to becoming men.

15.

Betty's Best Bourbon

DRINKING, DEATH, AND GRANDFATHERS were three things we did not talk about. For different reasons. Nobody drank. Not us boys, of course. But not them, either, the ones who were old enough to have the green cards, or whatever it took. There was a small exception maybe some years later when, coming in with the scythe on his shoulder, my father would have a cold beer and explain carefully that sometimes, when a person is really tired and has nothing else useful to do, a beer may, in those limited conditions, taste quite good. He seemed a little unsure about it in principle, but said he liked the taste when he finished especially sweaty work and when it was terrifically hot outside. This decision was clearly one of those matters of considerable moral import on which the family should stick together. In general, it was my position on most rules that they should be relaxed, since rules were mostly used by first or second sons to control third sons. Given the opportunity to strike a blow for the cause of fewer rules, one day I squared my shoulders and looked Don right in the eye and said that his decision to have a cold beer made sense to me, all right, it surely did.

But there were some limits in paradise. Nobody ever got tipsy. Getting angry was frowned on, too. Spending too much money on milk shakes and talking when silence would do just as well were discouraged.

Then again, some people had rules that we did not. Some people—and I believe these were people who frequented the less progressive parts of the state, probably cities, and especially mothers—had a rule against livestock in the kitchen. We did not have that rule.

It was a January morning and the thermometer read 25 degrees below zero Fahrenheit. I filled the buckets at the kitchen sink with steaming hot water and tromped out through the squeaky snow to the corral. It was a breath-white and eyebrows-frosted kind of morning. Hot water was used to melt the ice in the horse trough and the sheep's ice. Even the chickens had to have their water melted. When I got to the sheep pen in the barn, one of my large Corridale ewes was standing in the straw hovering over two wobbling baby lambs. The twins were still wet and looked like they were going to freeze. I ran back through the snow to the house. "I've got twin lambs! Their ears are freezing!"

"What?" said my mother. "You don't say!" Then she said, "Oh, my! On a day like this!" I said it was very cold and that the lambs' ears were turning black, that they were wet and we might lose them. My mother called the vet. The vet said, "Bring them inside and give them some whiskey."

It just so happened that at that very time my mother's beautiful cousin Betty, from New York, was visiting. Betty was from that part of the Schellenberg line that had never left the East Coast. She was slender and fine-featured in the way that I imagined eastern society ladies must be. Her husband, we were told, was a wealthy, proud executive in New York City. He stored people's old business papers more efficiently than anyone had ever stored them before and as a result had made quite a lot of money, which was pretty remarkable for anyone in our family. So my mother gave Betty a lot of credit for choosing wisely, and we all welcomed her to Arapahoe County with our best manners.

Betty did not share our side of the family's worries about the abuses of alcohol and tobacco. She chain-smoked and laughed with a husky gargle. Her laugh was deep-throated and warm and scratchy. She was what we in Arapahoe County would call a "woman of the world." At this moment she was still asleep. But she was a good bet for having the whiskey that the doctor had ordered.

I carried the lambs and led the ewe into the kitchen. We swaddled the twins in a pair of throwaway red and white flannel pajamas and laid them flat on the blue floor. They lay on their sides, wrapped to the necks, bleating pitifully, barely moving. The big ewe was a nervous wreck. She started out by messing up the floor. The kitchen was about ten feet long and four feet across, so there wasn't room for that, not really. When I got up to get a broom, I could not hold her and she rushed for the dining-room door and the rest of the house. Her hooves lost traction on the slick linoleum, and she slammed into the wood cupboards. "Watch for my china!" yelled my mother.

"Okay!" I yelled. The ewe rebounded, bouncing into the oven, which was hot. She tried to jump again but lost footing entirely and fell to her side on the floor. I grabbed her by the wool and pulled her skidding, bawling, and kicking sideways across the floor away from the danger. She struck the air with sharp cloven hooves. My mother edged backward and said, "I think we ought to keep this in the kitchen, don't you?" She edged over to close the door to the rest of the house.

For a moment everything was quiet. The two little lambs lay paralyzed in their flannels. My mother went to wake up Betty. It was late, probably about seven o'clock in the morning. New York people do not get up at the same time that people do who have responsibility for life and death in rural America. I waited on my knees, one arm around the neck of the ewe. The big sheep started bawling again and struggling, kicking, and wiggling, yowling like a stuck pig. At that moment, around the corner into the kitchen came Betty, blonde and elegant, in a flimsy silk negligee that had about as much substance as a cobweb in a dusty corner of the barn. The negligee fell thinly from her shoulders to her New York ankles. Her feet were bare, a flask was in her right hand, and she stared at the lambs and bawling ewe with a look of pure wonder. Nobody moved. After a while, Betty said, "Why, hel-*lo.*"

Immediately the ewe shut up. I did too, probably because my mouth was hanging open. I never before had had pink silk in my sheep pen. It seemed to me the woman might be just a tad cold.

"Well, we will need a spoon," my mother said.

"Oh, how lovely," Betty wheezed, and kneeled down beside the barely bleating lambs. "Oh, I'd love to. Yes, a spoon, please." She coughed with a rattle and bent over the tiny, woolly heads wrapped in red pajamas. "Here, baby," she said, lifting the head of one and wheezing with delight. "Oh, baby, here. Here, this is my very best bourbon!" Her pink negligee spread all over the blue linoleum in a great circle, filling the kitchen. She was like the Madonna of the lost sheep. While she was still down there on her knees, she started laughing, which turned to coughing, and then her gown fluttered above the lambs like some kind of heavenly pink snowstorm. My mother started laughing and held on to the stove to keep standing up. Betty ladled bourbon into each lamb until its soft brown eyes began to open. After that, when they began to wiggle, she unwrapped their maternity pajamas and they began to kick. My mother sighed, turned away, and made eggs and bacon for the human nursing corps. Betty got up and went to get dressed. The lambs scrambled to their feet and went looking for a substantial meal, poking their heads under the ewe.

Outside, the weather had warmed up to zero. "Good," my mother said, "that will be plenty warm." She called the vet. He said okay. Back to the barn. My mother approved. Betty was quite disappointed.

"Nobody in New York is going to believe this," she said.

"Well, you should come more often," my mother laughed. "It is always like this one way or another."

16.

A Liberal Education

ANY RESPECTABLE COUNTRY SCHOOL should have a bell tower, and ours did. Only we didn't have any bell. The building was just two rooms, above ground, for little kids and big kids, and one downstairs in the basement for in-between kids, my size. Nobody was supposed to like school, so I did my best to develop a negative attitude, but it was hard. Curtis School was not what anybody would call progressive, but it was personal. We covered everything from rattlesnake poison to Aphrodite, which Mrs. Fredrickson said were more or less the same thing. She said inside the county we had snakes, outside they had wily women. Both held practical challenges for the modern farm boy who had better watch out because, as bad as rattlers were, the world was even more dangerous once he crossed the county line.

Looking out from the school's front steps, there was nothing in any direction for a very long way except wheat fields, with the exception of the grange hall across the road, which was a center for important secret ceremonies.

We were glad to have a grange because it was a place where everybody said that our men stood up to be counted, which is certainly the right thing for a man to do. I did not know what they stood up to be counted for. "Well, that's why it's secret," said Erik, "to keep little kids from blabbing."

There was a deep artesian well right there at the back end of the schoolyard. Water flowed continually out of an old rusty pipe and spread along the road underneath elm trees that formed a green rectangle around the playground. They were the only shade for a half mile in any direction. But we had green elms and shade and an artesian well. "It's so deep that nobody knows how deep, but it's deeper than anything else around, you can bet," said Darryl, who walked with me to school every morning.

After a while the well went dry because good things come and go. "I knew it wouldn't last," said Darryl, who adjusted pretty fast, and who had an explanation for artesian wells and sudden calf deaths and UFOs. His father regularly drank a fair amount, especially on Saturdays and Sundays, and his big brother Dexter had a low-slung pink Chevy sedan that he liked to drive like a race car. Darryl said that his brother was accustomed to stopping for every second or third stop sign whether it was necessary or not.

Walking to school along the Highline Canal every morning, we mostly stayed away from talking about Darryl's dad or Dexter. There was just no cause to talk about that stuff. We made up dreams, heroes, and long passes for touchdowns that Darryl would throw someday down to Littleton, where people said Coach Gentile would not let any young man play football if he took to drinking. "Seems right," said Darryl, "because drinking don't help you none, not really, not to avoid tackles and not to avoid the next morning." I got the impression that there were a lot of next mornings that Darryl did not know what to do about. So that is how it was with us. Skirting along the road beneath the cottonwoods, rain or shine, we imagined how it would be some day, when we would probably be in charge of most of the long passes for the whole world.

My teacher was not gray-haired but I knew she was old. Her name was Mrs. Fredrickson, and when I got there she had been at that school twelve years, which was longer than I had been alive. Mrs. Fredrickson was among the oldest people I knew and I thought she was also one of the nicest. Upstairs, in the room above us, were the seventh, eighth, and ninth grades and Mrs. Post. She was really gray. She was principal. She was nice if you were good but she was not nice if you were bad, so I considered her dangerous because I could never tell if I was good enough.

Mrs. Fredrickson taught me the names of every state outside Colorado and all forty-eight capitals; she taught me the times tables and long division. She also taught me to water nasturtiums, at least, she said, if I wanted them to grow, and the names of all the birds of the West except for shorebirds, which we did not need because we did not have any shore.

She had to do some hard things, too. She put one of the kids, Denny, outside in the window well. He had to sit out there for a whole week in the October cold. He had stumbled into a skunk on the way to school, and she said it was not right for one smelly kid to destroy the concentration of the whole class. This was really true, but hard.

"It could happen anywhere," said Ed Weber sympathetically, who himself smelled a little like hogs and calves on some mornings. "Stumbling was not his fault," he said. Ed was also a stumbler. He stumbled just walking up to the blackboard. He was sympathetic to stumblers.

"No, it would not happen just anywhere, not really," said Arnie, laughing as if he had a trick up his sleeve. Arnie was athletic and never stumbled. "It would not happen in cities. You want to know why? It is because they don't have no skunks in cities. They already shot 'em all." Arnie was good at pointing out the progress that could be made in Western civilization with guns. So we were divided about Denny, who sat out there in the window well like a ghost, hovering in a thin blue windbreaker where he could hear class through the cracked window. But we could not smell him.

"He doesn't smell that bad," said Karen Weber, Ed's pretty sister, when Denny had been in exile about three days.

"Well, they should have washed him with tomato juice," replied Arnie. "That's what we did with Rex, the horse." He started laughing. "Or they could shoot him." He stuck his chin down into his chest and snickered, but no one paid Arnie any attention when he was mean.

"They can't afford to waste money on tomato juice," said Karen. "Have you seen that little one-room cinder-block house all eight of those kids live in? They can't just waste the juice just to get him out of the window well." She was right, of course. So we all wondered how Denny would manage with all those eight kids in that one-room cinder-block house, him smelling so bad. Maybe his parents put him outside at night just like Mrs. Fredrickson did during the day. Then somebody said, "Shhh! He can hear you," and no one said anything anymore.

Denny stayed at school for a while after his week in the window well and then he dropped out of Curtis School altogether. I think that getting hit by that skunk was pretty bad business, like when my grandfather lost his lumber mill to a fire. It is one of those things that can change a life forever. Denny was a really nice kid; always clean, hair combed, shirt tucked in when he arrived at Curtis in the morning. But after he went through that ordeal of being an outsider for a whole week, hearing us talking about him, I think he felt awkward and that maybe he was not so smart, so he stopped coming to school.

"Not smart to get hit by a skunk," said Arnie.

"Hasn't got anything to do with being smart," said Ed.

Smart had more to do with Roy Cooper, who was sixteen, long-boned and bulky, and still in the fifth grade. Roy had a hard time fitting under our fifth grade wooden desks, so he spent a fair amount of time when Mrs. Fredrickson was not looking carving under the desk with his knife, trying to make room for his legs. Which meant that the bottom shelf of his desk would no longer hold books so well, but that was not so important to Roy since he did not use books for anything but carrying. Roy was not dropping out on his own accord, but he was near to mandatory retirement. Mrs. Fredrickson tried to teach him to spell *Zeus* and *Argonaut*, which she said he might need to know someday. Roy was not so sure. He wondered out loud whether Jason and the Golden Fleece would be useful in crankshaft work.

He perked up a little when he saw pictures of Aphrodite floating around without so many clothes on, but calmed down again when Mrs. Fredrickson got back to Odysseus, even though, as she pointed out, he was busy floating from one island goddess to the next. "Life is a journey," she said, trying to hook him. "Everyone who thinks that he is at home is maybe going to have to go on a journey sometime. Goddesses, monsters, adventures are all out there. We are all on a wine-dark sea. We are all like Odysseus."

"Can we get back to the goddess?" asked Roy.

In truth, Mrs. Fredrickson often said she believed that not everybody needs to know math, either, but the state made her teach everyone everything. She said she looked forward to the day when the rules changed and not everyone had to study everything. At home, my father said Mrs. Fredrickson could be wrong because everybody really did need to know math, including me. I liked Mrs. Fredrickson's position better, but she did not worry me as much as my father did, so I studied math and Roy studied about the great journey in search of the Golden Fleece and we met all the state's requirements.

Mrs. Fredrickson also taught us to sing "Over the River and Through the Woods," which she said we needed because it was traditional and therefore good, and "Harbor Lights," which was right to the edge of being dangerously modern. She was a very balanced person. I liked "Harbor Lights" and offered that maybe this was a song about Odysseus. I wanted to sing the romantic part, hand to the chest, eyes to the sky, but she never picked me to sing solo because she said Hap Tanner—who was only a fourth grader for God's sake and probably did not even know what romance was—and Arnie Coughlin both were more likely to stay in tune. This was a surprise to me because I thought maybe that since I could do all the journeys of Odysseus better than anyone, I might be able to sing better, too. I also did not like it that Mrs. Fredrickson seemed secretly pleased that she could pass the blessings around to everyone. I thought maybe if I did not raise my hand so much in class, she would call on me to sing. I could tell people who sang well were more popular than people who knew about Odysseus.

There were about seven of us in my class. So it was natural to raise my hand a lot; there were not many other people who were going to do that. Louise Elmore did sometimes. She was very smart, small and demure, and came from a white house in a big wheat field that was flanked by two lonely elm trees. The two trees were gray, black from October to April and that was all the beauty there was over there. Everything else at her place was outbarns and haystacks and dirt and mowers and broken-down fence. Louise's brother was a swagger bully and her father was dark and withdrawn. Louise was glad to be in school, I think. She wore little flimsy pink and white cotton dresses that had been washed so often there was hardly any pattern or thickness left in them. I don't think there was much money over there under the two elms because Louise had a choice of about two dresses and, since the color was gone, they looked pretty much alike.

Then there was Roy, who never raised his hand, ever. And Ed Weber, who was thinking more about pigs and alfalfa than about Zeus and the Argonauts, and his twin sister Karen, who was pretty and pink-cheeked but did not like either Zeus or math. Finally, there was Denny, who got hit by the skunk, and Arnie, who would sooner fight than answer any school question. That was the fifth grade.

Sixth-grade girls spent most of their time passing lipstick back and forth, up and down their row. They were pretty excited about being beautiful and getting old, which they were, because they were the oldest in our whole room. Upstairs, in the room for grades seven through nine, though, there were some girls, even older, who did not play ball or run-around games during recess because they were busy on the steps practicing kissing. I could hardly look at that, although Lavonne, one of those girls, was plenty good-looking and I could see she had a fine future in kissing.

Sometimes during the dry season, Ed, Arnie, Darryl, and the others hung out at the artesian well and told stories. They talked about before the war when wheat brought less per bushel "down to Littleton at the silo" than it did by our time, or about the Dust Bowl when there was nothing out there but wind and brown clouds.

Sometimes they teased about the farmer who plowed around and around the same hill until the upper two legs on his horse got shorter than the lower two legs. The older boys lollygagged around in the sun of May and threw rocks at big red ants, which they called "piss ants," but which I could not say because we did not talk like that in our family.

One time I did not go to school because one of my hens was hatching chicks in the casket case in the barn. I went out that morning and found little cracks breaking out in the eggs and tiny pink beaks wedging up through them. Those eggs didn't all get laid on the same day, but somehow all those chicks were coming out on the same day. I was excited and said to my mother that it could be very educational to find out why this was, and she arched her eyebrow and said why yes, she was sure that might be true, and let me spend the day scrunched down in the casket case watching. The casket case was just the right size to stretch out in and watch underneath the hen. She wasn't supposed to nest in there, of course, since mostly we used it to store grain, but once a hen starts to brood you have got to leave her there.

Whenever a cracked brown egg rolled out of the nest or a little chick could not get clean from the shell that stuck to it, I helped by peeling little bits off its fuzzy wet down. I made sure the chicks stayed warm under the hen and that none of them were out in the cold. Next morning the note from my mother to Mrs. Fredrickson said, "Please excuse Craig; he was in the casket case with the chickens." Usually, all you had to do to get out of school was to be sick with scarlet fever or mumps, so I figured that since I was already in the casket it was a cinch I would be excused. Anyway, my mother may have thought new chicks were as big a mystery as the Golden Fleece. Or maybe her handwriting was so bad that Mrs. Fredrickson never knew what she said and it didn't matter, anyway.

Chickens hatched so seldom that most of the time I had to study Jason and Aphrodite. Once a week Mrs. Fredrickson summoned the fifth grade to the back table. Fourth grade would have been over in their two rows doing arithmetic problems; over in the sixth the very sophisticated girls would be comparing lipsticks and passing notes, which, I believe, is what girls of that age are best at. Ed and Karen Weber were at the back table with Roy Cooper, Louise and Arnie, and for a while, Denny. We were not for the most part natural Jason followers. Still, we all memorized how to spell *Hera* and *Aphrodite* and learned that if a person sows dragon's teeth in the soil in a certain part of the world—probably outside of Arapahoe County—he will get a fine, fully equipped army with swords, spears, and shields growing right up out of the ground. So we were not naive; we knew about the real world.

One time we were supposed to plant some nasturtium seeds in a pot with dirt and water and some in a pot that we would not water. It was an experiment to show the value of watering plants. I would have thought we knew that without having to make an experiment out of it. But I raised my hand to volunteer, as usual, and Mrs. Fredrickson asked me to be the person to write the labels for the pots. I wrote, "Pea Pot with Water" and "Pea Pot without Water," just like I thought she had said, and taped the labels to the sides of the two pots. My brother Erik, who was not minding his own business for some reason, came downstairs from his plush and sunny upstairs classroom—which had all the windows and where they certainly had plenty of assignments to do on their own without making trouble for others—and just happened to walk into our classroom and see my labels. He started laughing. He was holding his sides and harrumphing. He was ridiculous.

"*Pee* pot with water?" he laughed out loud so the whole class could hear.

Mrs. Fredrickson stood nearby watching him. She clamped her jaw down and tried to keep from smiling. She was a nice person. She was not an uncultured, limp-minded lout.

That night at the dinner table, I complained about certain louts of my direct acquaintance who I could mention, if asked.

"*Whom* I could mention," my father said with a twinkle in his eye. "When it is the object it takes a 'whom'."

"Limp-minded louts 'whom' I could mention," I said, scowling across the table.

There was a pause. Frank started laughing. Erik looked at his peas and started laughing, and then my mother started laughing. They were making it hard for me to stay focused. This is the kind of problem a small person has who wants to be serious and no one else in the house cares.

So I gave it up and got on with life, which is what my father told me to do. This meant I had to get up and take my turn at washing dishes, which I decided was more or less my final fate, anyway. Sometimes school at Curtis was easier than school at the dinner table. At least at Curtis I didn't have to do the dishes when I was right. "It's a hard life," said my mother, handing me the pots.

One April day a herd of us boys was standing by the artesian well in the shade under the elms and Roy Cooper said, "Daylight savings don't make that much sense, really, because I always feed and water in daylight, whether it is five or six o'clock, don't matter." That made sense to me. I never could figure out why the clock changed.

I said, "A person can track his way to summer by noticing how much brighter it is just at getting-up time, and a person can think, if this keeps up, it will be vacation soon."

When Roy made his comment, I was thinking that there would soon be green in the alfalfa fields and water in the irrigation ditch and wood-chip boats to race down the feeder canal. I was thinking of summer and green leaves and long sunsets. I was thinking that when someone back east changes the clock, puts it forward, it upsets my whole progress toward Fair time. So I was with Roy in spirit even if I was just making up things to say.

Roy said it had to be someone who "lives in the dark between skyscrapers," and who "probably never even seen the sun." I kicked the dirt and threw a stone at piss ants crawling over their red nest, and said I thought that was probably right. Of course, I really did not think that, because I had been to a lot of cities and knew that there was sun in there. But I wanted to agree with Roy. He was always on the outside of things everywhere and I felt bad for knowing so much about Zeus when he never could answer a single question from Mrs. Fredrickson.

Ed Weber must have felt the same way. He said, "Maybe city people need time to play golf in the afternoon, since they have no chores at all." Ed had probably never seen a golf club in his entire life but said, "If a person don't have to milk, he probably could play golf in all that extra sun in the afternoon." This was as close to being envious as Ed could get.

Arnie said, "Bring one of those daylight savings guys out here and I could use a golf club to pound some sense into him." You had to know Arnie to know that he was trying to support Roy, too; it was just that his way of helping was usually to want to shoot somebody.

"Arnie is always thinking about pounding someone," said Darryl. "He don't know who's doing what to who, not really." I did not correct Darryl or make him say, "Who's doing what to *whom*," because a lot of times dinner-table learning was not very valuable at the artesian well.

In the fall, we played touch football two hands below the waist and got ready to play the wealthy kids in Cherry Hills. They lived over on the north side of Belleview, which could have been another world. They lived where the houses, lawns, and trees were big, and there were maples and willows instead of cottonwoods, and no irrigation ditches except to feed their magnificent golf course. They lived in another zone, is what they did; we didn't have cherry, walnut, or chestnut trees on our side of Belleview and we knew that. "Nice people," my mother said about them sometimes. "Nice people" was a phrase reserved for strangers. No matter how close they lived, the Cherry Hills people were on the other side of the paved road and even though some of them were "nice people," this was still arm's length. Sometimes, when my mother was surprised, she said certain wealthy people she knew were "real" people, which was her way of saying that, for a few of them, being rich was not necessarily a permanent disadvantage. But we knew that it wasn't easy getting over being rich; you had to work at it. You had to work at being real.

We learned one autumn during one of those football games against Cherry Hills that you can fool rich kids with an end-around reverse once, but not twice in a row. They may be slow but they are not that slow. Darryl was the most talkative person in school, and the best-looking athlete, so he was our quarterback. He was also a grade older, sixth grade, and therefore smarter. He was calling signals. We were out in the back field by the artesian well. Six farm boys lined up in the dust on one side; six good-looking, scrubbed sons of bankers and real estate brokers lined up on the other. Lavonne and Kathleen were cheerleaders for us. They had interrupted kissing practice to come out and root for the boys, mostly Darryl. Maybe they figured that boys have to win some big victory first before you can kiss them, so this was important; this was part of their long-term plan to get heroes like Odysseus. They didn't have uniforms. It didn't matter. Lavonne wore pretty skirts and loved to jump up and down and yell, "Go Darryl!" Louise was a sort of cheerleader, too. She was a quiet person and didn't yell at all, ever. She could spell Zeus—Z-E-U-S—at the back table during mythology class but she never could yell. But she smiled and that was good enough for me, and with her and Lavonne and Kathleen, we didn't pay any attention to the girls who came from Cherry Hills because they were not ours, and besides they were too extraordinarily good-looking and well-dressed to be real.

Darryl sometimes got into trouble for talking too much in class but on the football field his talking was a good thing. He could set the rules just by being loud. "Kick ova!" he yelled when the other side kicked out of bounds and it was too close to our goal for comfort. One small thing about Darryl, though, was that he was not so good at pronouncing Rs, which could be a problem for certain plays. "Go wight!" he might whisper in the huddle, or "Wewerse!" Then we stood there staring at him. "Wewerse wight!" he whispered again, so low we could barely hear. We all ran out of the huddle and up to the ball where it was lying in the dirt, thinking, *Oh, boy, I hope someone else knows what to do.*

"Hut! Hut! Hut! Hut!" Darryl yelled at the top of his lungs, so loud that Kathleen and Lavonne stopped gossiping under the elms and watched the action. Everybody but I knew what to do and the reverse worked. Hand-off to Erik, hand-off to Arnie, around right end. Ten yards and dust and sticks and shouts and then calm. Next, Darryl called a double reverse and it worked, too. Hand-off to Erik, hand-off to Arnie, and then hand back to Darryl going the other way. Ten more yards through a cloud of dust. That got us to midfield, which was halfway between the artesian well and the feeder ditch, which were the goal lines.

But then we bogged down. Arnie got out of hand. He was having so much fun knocking rich kids into the dust that he got penalized for unnecessary roughness. After that, we could never make the double reverse work or get past the fifty-yard line. It was not Arnie's fault, really. He did a lot of haying in summers, milked every morning and night, and had arms like steel pipes. Darryl said Arnie was used to getting hit at home by all the men in the family who were bigger than him. He was the youngest in that house and the only thing he ever got trained to do over there was swing at people. So when Arnie finally found someone even younger and smaller running right at him, he just lifted an elbow to the chin and took the poor banker child out.

Arnie and Roy Cooper were supposed to be blockers. Roy liked being uncorked from underneath his wooden desk in the basement, and he was a natural just because he could stick a long leg in front of anybody for yards around. The kids from Cherry Hills felt like they either had to go around by way of Kansas or run into a wall. But Arnie was something else. He thought of himself as a sort of destroyer, so he went out of his way to find city people to knock down. When he came back to the huddle after he got penalized, nobody said anything. Arnie was looking red-faced and pretty dangerous. Anybody who said anything might get decapitated. So after that, we spent as much time trying not to run into Arnie, on our side, as we did trying to run away from the boys on the other side. It was no wonder we had a tough time going forward.

Ed Weber, the son of the pig farmer, was also there. He was not very fast or very smooth, or very anything, but he was one of the nicest people on the planet, so we always asked him to play center so he could at least touch the ball. He was one of those guys who would wander into a bloody nose without half trying and then just smile and say he was okay. His feet flapped when he walked, and if anything was around to stumble on, he found it.

We were bogged down at the fifty-yard line and then Darryl threw a pass. A twelve-year-old future stock-broker from Cherry Hills got in the way and batted the ball high up into the air. Ed Weber was somehow, by this time, all alone over by the sideline. He probably went over there to get a handkerchief for his bloody nose. Everybody watched the ball float through the air toward Eddie, who turned around just in time to see it coming. He stood flat-footed, opened his arms, and smiled. The ball floated down square on his chest and he hugged it. Lavonne screamed and jumped up and down, and we all yelled "Run, Ed, run!" He looked around toward the goal line. There was no one near him. He cranked his arms and bent his head and ran for about ten yards and then, without any help, his right foot got caught up in his left foot and Eddie crashed face into the dirt. Lavonne's screaming must have knocked him over. The play ended. No touchdown. It didn't matter. Ed got up grinning from ear to ear and laughing. Everybody else was laughing and yelling for joy and Lavonne yelled, "Good, Eddie!" just like she did for Darryl.

The game ended zero to zero. After we ran out of reverses, we didn't have any other trick plays. The real estate and banker boys could never find a way to run around Arnie and Roy. So everybody ran up and down in the dust a lot, but nobody was as good at making things work as they were at making things not work for the other side. Nobody scored and at the end of the game it was still farm kids zero, rich kids zero.

Arnie figured it was a case of us being tougher, farm kids, and them being smarter, rich kids. So it was classic brawn against brains, and it had come out even. "Which means you don't have to be smart, not really," he said hopefully. He repeated this hope the next day when we got back into class with Mrs. Fredrickson. He said that we surely were tougher than those other boys and that we should have won except for some bad officiating, but at least we came out even, which means it is just as good to be strong as it is to be smart. Mrs. Fredrickson smiled rather noncommittally at Arnie and then looked away down the row at Ed Weber, who was sitting in the back. "I saw you catch that pass," she said. "Good, Eddie." Then she filled the room with a smile reserved for kings and princes. "*Good,* Eddie," she repeated softly. Eddie didn't say anything but shuffled his feet under his wood desk. After a while he looked up again and everybody was still looking at him. He grinned but didn't say anything.

Later, when it was time to go back to the table to talk about Greek myths, Eddie was the first one there, book open, ready to go. "Let's talk about the Golden Fleece," he said.

17.

Skills for the Modern Man

ONE OF THE STEPS TO BECOMING a full-fledged man was
to learn how to rock climb. Erik taught me, more or less.
He was in high school, and by that time, it was either
learn rock climbing or go out with girls, so he learned
climbing, which he figured was a whole lot safer. Or
maybe he thought the way to a girl's heart was to save
her in a blizzard on the Eiger. He was reading a book
called *The White Tower* about heroics in the Swiss Alps,
and there were stars in his eyes when he said, "Boy,
Craig, you ought to read this!" I was interested because
there were heroics involved, daring rescues on sheer
faces in sudden August storms; lives saved, lives lost.

Erik got the mountaineering catalogues and bought
all kinds of slick nylon rope and carabiners and wedges
and hammers and came out of his room with words like
rappel and *belay* and said he needed someone to do it
with. I was not interested in saving some girl in a blizzard, but Frank was by now safely in his senior year and
he already had a girlfriend, so Erik looked around for

somebody else in the living room he could practice on. He needed someone he could dangle from a rope and study to see if he was doing it right. There was not a single candidate left but me.

So we started out on the chimney. If a person was very careful, Erik said—he always emphasized "a person" when the entity was sort of expendable, like a bag of grain or a stranger from the East—he could climb up by stepping off the back doorknob, spread-eagle over onto the first jutting bricks of the chimney, and then scale up, notch by notch, to reach the roof. He thought this was quite neat. I thought this was quite high. "Then," he said, when we were standing on the gray tar shingles looking fifteen feet down to the stone patio below, "the fun thing is to dangle off the back of the chimney and see if you can get down."

We did this for a few days and I began to get the knack of it. Then one day Don came home from work and wondered out loud how it happened that the chimney seemed to be pulling away from the house. "Why, look there," he said. "There seems to be an inch or two showing between the bricks and the wood frame. I never noticed that before." Erik moved his ropes to under the bed and then at dinner he fessed up.

After that, we had to go find the best cottonwood on the canal and see if we could rappel off one of those big trees. This was not something I could say I was learning to love. But there was a lot to be said for being available and learning whatever it is that comes your way, especially when you are in the eighth grade and in need of prestige wherever you can find it. When we got

to the cottonwoods, there was no back-door handle to
start the climb with, and the only way we could get up
off the ground was to find a tree that leaned over like
the Tower of Pisa. If we could find a giant, rough-barked
tree that was sloping at an angle, we could scramble up
the flat side and rappel back down. It would be almost
like a real mountain, a sort of branchy Eiger Peak. Or
that was the idea. Erik demonstrated it just fine. I
climbed up okay, but when it was time to rappel, I
stepped off with the rope around my neck and crotch
and within about two steps down, it was just around my
neck. I lost my footing on the flat side of the tree and
swung around to the underside where there was nothing
to keep my feet on. I was hanging out in the air, the rope
firmly around my neck and nowhere near my seat,
twirling in space. Erik came running up, laughing, and I
laughed with my eyes but not with my mouth because
the rope was squishing my vocal cords. Since I was only
about three feet off the ground, he shouldered up underneath my tail end and hefted me into the air so I could
lift the rope from around my neck. Then we fell into the
prairie grass and leaves, heaving laughter, and me saying, *Okay, I think I've got that one.*

Then he thought we needed a real mountain, and
we went up Bear Creek Canyon until he found just the
right-looking sheer-faced, rocky cliff. "It's got to be the
right stone," he said, "else our pitons will pull out." The
cliff we were looking at was sandstone. "It's not so
good," he said. "Too soft to hold the pitons." But we
were already up there, and we were carrying all this
expensive nylon rope around our shoulders and looked

ready for Everest, or at least the Eiger, so he said, "It's not so steep, anyway. Let's scale up the easy part and rappel down the cliff face. There is a pine tree on the top that can hold us just fine, and we won't have to depend upon pitons in the loose rock."

So we took about an hour to climb up the face of the cliff and get around to where the pine tree was, right out on the edge of a sheer drop. "Perfect," Erik said. He roped up and dropped over the edge, but the tree was on the outcrop of a big overhang and I could not see him, so I did not know what he was doing under there. He did not shout or cry out or anything, so I figured he was all right, and in about twenty minutes, there he was seventy-five yards away, down on the canyon floor, waving. He was exultant. "Okay!" he yelled, "come on down!" I looked over the edge, thinking, *Well, he did it, it must be okay.* "Just take it easy, Craig!" he yelled. "Go slow and you will be fine!" He didn't say anything about the overhang.

It is part of being the youngest to have faith. So I looped the rope around the pine tree, then wrapped both strands around my leg, up through the crotch, across my chest, around the right side of my neck, and under my left arm, and I looked over the cliff. In my left hand I held the uphill strands that came from around back of my neck. In my right hand I held the long end of the rope that came down through my legs and across my chest. There was about a thirty-foot drop into open air, but back underneath the tree roots, about five feet in, was a sheer, white sandstone wall. I could not reach the wall face with my legs, but I had to get back there for a proper rappel. I didn't think about it very hard and didn't cinch the rope up as tight as I could have. Erik had done it easy, and once I got to the wall I knew it would be like coming down the chimney. Nothing to it. So I just stepped out into the air with about five feet of loose rope between my right hand and the tree.

I fell cleanly for all five feet, hit the end of the rope, and snapped inward like a human pendulum, smack against the sandstone wall. *Thump.* Or maybe more like *crack.* My feet dangled beneath me and the rope tightened around my neck. My face was flat on the stone. I could taste the rock and a little blood in my mouth. *That was dumb,* I thought. *Must be something I didn't do quite right.* Face, arms, hands, and knees were yelling pain, but I hung on.

"You okay?" Erik yelled up from way down on the canyon floor. He was laughing and worried at the same time. "You okay?"

"Yeah, yeah, okay," I gargled and spit out, trying to haul my feet up against the cliff wall so that I could use the rope to get leverage around my legs and bottom instead of my neck. "Okay. Okay . . ." I inched my legs up under me, ignored the throbbing all over, and finally got my knees in front of my chest so I could push out against the rock, rope across the chest and through the legs. I lunged with my weight and pulled the rope away from the burn, which now creased raw around the back side of my neck. Slowly, I eased down the rope to flat ground.

"Man," I said, legs wobbling, trembling, "that was dumb. I just stepped off into the air."

"Yeah," he said. "I should have told you. You got to get your legs to the wall." We drove down the canyon toward home. "These are skills," he said hopefully, "that could come in handy sometime."

I tried and tried to think about just when that would be. He wanted me to like it. I wanted to, too. But, man. . . .

It could have been about this time that I began to think that as dangerous as girls were, they might be safer than I had thought, and they had to be safer than some things.

18.

Death of the Highline King

I FELL IN LOVE WITH LOUISE ELMORE. It was a necessary part of getting old, I guess. But no one paid much attention, including Louise. We would hover around comparing arithmetic scores at recess at Curtis School. She was also good in spelling. I was pretty good there, too; better than in math. So we were naturals, really, companions in the art of performance at the big table in the back of the room. Louise couldn't sing either, so we both knew rejection, which is good for mature relationships. But there was always one thing or another: hay to put up, or ditch to clean, or sheep to take out to graze. So this romance does not really count as one of the major disasters of my young life.

It was a lot more serious when Ed Weber's brother got polio. All over the state there was a big epidemic. Nobody was supposed to go swimming. It was summer-hot and sweltering under the cottonwoods, one of those times when heat radiates up out of the dirt and stones and even the wood in the corral poles. It didn't matter. *Stay away from the public pools,* said all the city mothers who lived where there were public pools, and even the country mothers—who generally raise very considerable children—agreed we should stay out of the Highline Canal.

"You never know what could be in there," said my mother. She was thinking of the dead sheep that we saw once every couple of years.

"Really," we said to her, "there are hardly ever any dead sheep." But she did not relent and we sweated out that summer, dry and hot.

Not far from the house there was a big cottonwood branch that hung way out over the canal. In normal times we filled a gunnysack with straw and dangled it from a rope out over the water. Then we could pull the gunnysack toward the bank and leap on and swing out in death-defying arcs over the current, leaping back onto the bank at the top of the return swing. Or sometimes, to prove to lesser city friends that we were brave beyond human measure, we would swing out and drop into the icy-cold, snow-melted water and battle the current to swim ashore. The water was about four feet deep and dark brown, and whatever was under the surface was a pure guess. Still, this was a test of manhood that meant the difference between those who would probably succeed in life and those who might not or who would have to become indoor people, maybe even bankers.

"Swing on that thing and you could end up paralyzed stiff as a board," said Erik, who saw me looking longingly at the gunnysack where it hung motionless above the water. I knew he was right and I didn't do it.

And then Ed's brother got it.

Ed and Karen came to school one day all ashen and quiet, and the smile that was always on Ed's face was gone. They were both scared to death and with good reason. As it turned out, their older brother never walked again.

For a long time Ed Weber's brother was the nearest we came to thinking about dying. He went into an iron lung and day by day things never changed with him. Then Darryl's brother Dexter who, as I said earlier, was used to stopping at every other stop sign, got caught by the sheriff. Well, he almost got caught. The sheriff saw him miss a stop sign and tried to catch him. Dexter pumped his foot down on the gas pedal. Darryl said later, wistfully, "He just taken out of there." Dexter came hurtling down the hill in his pink Chevy headed south out of Cherry Hills, and when he crossed Belleview he left the last pavement and hit the gravel road. He went smoking up the hill about three quarters of a mile from our kitchen window, scattering gravel and rocks as he went. My mother said real loud so we could hear in the living room, "Uh-oh, there goes somebody in a pink Chevy with sirens right behind."

I guess we all knew the only pink Chevy for miles around, but we never said Dexter's name, not any of us, because there was a chance we were wrong. For sure, it looked like pain and trouble for the Bartlemes, right down the road. Better to keep quiet and hope for the best.

Dexter raced on up out of sight of our window until we couldn't see him anymore, but we could still hear the sirens when he went over the hill past Curtis School a mile away. He ignored the last stop sign between him and Douglas County, probably thinking one more sign violation was not going to make much difference. It was probably the last conscious, fully rational decision he was to make in his life, and it was the wrong one. He was going awfully fast when he went up past our kitchen window and he sure hadn't slowed down any when he went past Curtis. Maybe he figured he could outmaneuver the sheriff on the dirt roads in his own home territory. The road up there hits the winding part of the Highline Canal and turns. Maybe Dexter figured he could zip a left or a right and scoot down under the cottonwoods and let the sheriff sail past. But he never made it around the first turn.

Where the road bends to the canal his wheels lost traction in the gravel. He got about forty-five degrees around the bend and then took to the air and floated out over the canal until he hit a cottonwood. They swept him up and ambulanced him to the hospital, where he hung in a coma for weeks while everybody prayed and whispered and talked about him being close to passing on.

Finally, Darryl started to give me reports on days when we were walking along the ditch toward school. "He's going to have to start ova," Darryl said, "because he ain't neva going to be able to talk and think like he used to." In the end Dexter lived but never again talked so well, and his days of clear thinking were over. It seemed like the families at Curtis were getting about all the trouble they needed for one year.

Then one day that same summer, a girl I didn't know too well came hurrying around the bend of the ditch driving a big buckskin horse at full speed, holding on tight, looking kind of pale. She reined to a quick halt beside

Erik and me, who were standing beside the big cotton-wood looking longingly at the gunnysack over the water in the canal. The girl was riding an English saddle, which never does give a person much to hold on to, anyway, and she seemed nervous as could be. She was one of those people from the other side of Belleview who had very pretty horses and rode English, which was not a crime really, but it was like people who did not wear Levi's. They were from a whole different world. She said that there was something wrong down at the Big Bend, that there was a man in a car. She said she was going on home right away, and we had better do something about it.

There was a pretty good chance that since this girl rode English, she scared easy; she might not have the real western makings. So Erik and I thought we could look the situation over without any risk to ourselves. We quickly bridled Chita and Captain and galloped bare-back down toward the Big Bend to see what we could see. I could have avoided that and had an okay life. But I didn't. There was this man sitting in the front seat, his face all pale and cold as a ghost. I had never seen anything so awful. The engine was running and a hose went from the exhaust to the front window beside his head. The window was rolled up so that there was just enough room for the hose to stick in beside his face. All the rest of the windows were closed. *Chug, chug, chug* went the engine. From forty feet away, which was as close as we got, any person could tell this man was dying or dead.

We took one long wide-eyed look. I sucked in my breath and went all cold inside. Erik did not say anything, but I think he was going numb like I was. "Let's get out of here," he said. We jerked our horses around toward home and galloped hell-bent for leather toward the white house. We reported to my mother, who called the emergency number. Within about fifteen minutes a red fire engine from Littleton and about twenty volunteer fireman's cars came bumping and lurching down our little two-wheel track of a ditch road toward the Big Bend. The firemen did whatever they did, but I did not go down there. And whatever they did, it did not help any. Pretty soon the whole string of cars came back, inching forward, headlights at first going by, then red taillights disappearing into the gloom of night, headed home toward Littleton. It was all over for them and for whoever had been in that car. I wish it had been all over for me, but it wasn't even close.

Generally, when I was not out under the cottonwoods, I slept in a room in a far corner of the basement. That meant I had to walk through the dark from one end of the house, where the basement stairs came down, to the other end, where there was a light for my room. It meant feeling my way about fifty feet through the basement between boxes and around corners until I came to the light switch at my end. It took about fifteen seconds in the pitch dark and always made me nervous.

That night, I would not venture a foot down those stairs. I hovered around inside the house, scared of the dark, scared to go outdoors, scared to move away from the living room, not wanting to talk, an image of the dead man's face burned into my brain. I slept on the couch as close to my parents as I could get. I did not say I was afraid, but I was a wreck. My head hurt, my legs hurt, and I was twitching scared all night long. I tossed and turned and saw that pale ghostly face in my mind like a picture that would never go away. Nobody could say anything to help. Every time I closed my eyes, there the white face was: closed eyes, droopy jaw.

The newspaper reported next day that the man's name was Carlos Rhea. Neither I nor anybody in my family had ever heard of him. But neither the name nor the face ever faded. For weeks I could not sleep, and I would not go into the basement room. When I did, I trembled down there in fear. We didn't talk about it much. Erik was doing the same thing, moping around, keeping quiet. I think it bothered him quite a lot, too. But what could anyone do to erase the face imprinted on our brains? My mother was sympathetic, but she couldn't crawl in there and wash out my head. There was nothing to do.

I didn't want to go near the Big Bend anymore. I didn't want to be down there alone, stalking the ground squirrels, lying in the dust, watching magpies. For four or five years before that time, Stormy and I used to work our way through the buckbrush and tall grass, and we knew every secret ledge and trail. I knew the holes in the trees where the woodpeckers lived. I knew where you could hide, unseen, from a plowing tractor when it was only fifteen feet away. I knew the mouse trails in the grass, the larger squirrel trails, the prairie-dog towns, the places where pheasants hide. I knew who else lived in my community, and secretly, every few months, not to show off but to state a fact, I drew a circle in the mud with the letters HK in the middle. "HK" stood for "Highline King." I knew that this act was arrogant. So I did not tell anyone except the dog Stormy. He was part of the Highline brotherhood. We were caretakers, and he understood. I didn't tell anyone else. Not Darryl. Not even Erik. I just knew that for a mile between our road and the next one, these cottonwoods, these wheel tracks, this buckbrush, and the squirrel trails through the wild grass were my domain. I was the Highline King.

But after Carlos Rhea died at the Big Bend, I never made that claim anymore; I never drew the circle in the mud again. That suicide made it not my place. My cottonwood home had been invaded. It had been wrecked by an unthinking man who thought he had gone far away where he could be alone. He was not far away from anywhere; he was at the very center of my world, and he turned it from lovely and safe into something fearful, perilous, and dark. "He ruined it," I murmured secretly to Stormy. The dog and I were lying on the floor and I had my head on his side, face into his soft black and white fur. The rest of the family was scattered in chairs around the room, reading. No one could see my eyes. "It's over," I whispered again. "He ruined it." Stormy's fur absorbed my tears. The dog raised his head, thumping his tail on the floor; he was ready to go for a run again, anytime. But I did not go with him. Not then, not for a long time. It was not safe out there.

We killed pigs and chickens for eating, and I never did question death for those purposes. It was, all the old people said, part of what a person had to learn. But Carlos Rhea, without ever knowing me, had shattered my paradise. Ed's brother's polio pretty much shattered the happiness of the Weber family, and Darryl's brother's car crash pretty much did the same for him and his family. It was a bad year.

19.

Natural Gold

SOMETIMES THINGS HAPPEN that are okay. I knew that. My mother would come along in the late afternoon and praise the golden sky as the sun drifted down over Mount Evans. She would see gold in the dirt in her garden and gold in the leaves of October and smile and make sure that we all appreciated things that shine, things that glow, things that are alive. She did her best.

At school I went into seventh grade and met Mrs. Post. She was a battle-ax. Sometimes she smiled. But mostly she was a battle-ax. She was very high on thinking. "Think, think think," she said. With her there was no little fluff of nonsense around the edges as there had been with Fredrickson. If Post had an apron—highly unlikely—it would have had a straight-lined pattern, no flowers, black and white.

Well, maybe some blue. No pink. We never once had a fight on her watch at Curtis School. Post said to us that the weather and luck are enough to grind a man down; we don't have to do it to each other. She said that in wheat country thrashing is universal; wheat and people both get it sometime, just without trying. *Even golden wheat,* she said, *has to get thrashed, and so do golden people, but you don't have to do it on my watch.*

When she said that, I twitched. I did not like the idea of getting thrashed on my way to being golden. Once she even said, "Boys and girls, it's math time! Time for the thrashing!"

I was scared of math. My father, Frank, and Erik were easy at it, like fish in water. I would listen, at home at night, to my father explaining decimal points, and wonder if maybe there was some option to everything so precise. What was clear to him was a lot of options to me. I was better at gray than at black and white.

One day when we were grading papers—we always graded our own—I cheated. I changed my answer. When we got back to the table in the back of the room, Post found the change on my paper. She went black, deep and dark like the eye of a prairie thunderhead before a cloudburst. I sat there like a prisoner in the dock.

I knew Post had never experienced this problem with my two older brothers. Now, to her surprise, "little Barnes" was a different Barnes. He cheated. She probably thought he cheated all the time. She probably thought he cheated at home on his allowance. She probably thought he liked killing chickens and charging too much for the eggs he sold. She would know a born felon when she saw one.

She went dark and I went pale and thought my life was over. Of all the bad days after Carlos Rhea's death, this was just about as bad. Now I was no longer scared of just the outside world; I was scared of myself.

I had been afraid, that summer and fall, to go outside in the dark. I was afraid to feed and water the stock when dusk started to settle around the barn. I was afraid in other ways, too, like to be wrong about anything. I was afraid to be wrong in school. I was afraid to be wrong in math. So I changed my test score and I got caught. Carlos Rhea took away the ditch and the hawks and the pheasants and the golden grain in the world around me. My cheating took away something I could count on in myself.

Post did not do anything, really. She just said something like, "Sometimes, we just have to be right, don't we?" There was silence around the table. Louise was shocked. She was the smartest and the nicest and she must have thought that I would never do that sort of thing. Now she knew I was bad, like everyone else. Arnie was happy. He beamed. Dean Milligan, a new kid, would now know, I realized, exactly who I was, too. A cheater. The silence was awful. Post did not say another word, but disappointment dripped from her like wax from a candle.

That day I went home and did not tell anyone. That night I did not sleep again; I let people just think I was still scared about the suicide. I lay in my bed and sweated.

Days went on like this. I never did tell anyone. Not ever. Not until this very day. September passed on into October. My mother reveled in the golden leaves of the great cottonwoods and my father in the joy of a good formula or a solution to a quadrilateral equation, and I walked through time like a wooden man, a dry skin without nerves. Once in a while in the old casket case in the barn we would find a shriveled-up dead mouse that had got in there and could not get out again. The skin would be all dry and wrinkled and stiff. I went through the fall feeling like one of those dead mice.

The buckbrush under the cottonwoods turned copper and gray and the grass along the ditch lay down cream-colored. I walked home from school along the canal kicking leaves in the long grass and wanted more than ever to be an actor somewhere, to be a king somewhere, to be good at something.

In the middle of October, Erik shot a skunk out in Savage's wheat field and a couple of weeks later rode Smoky out, put a rope around the carcass, and dragged it to Judy Shomp's house. He left it on the front doorstep as a sign of his affection. Judy was something special to Erik, but he had spent too much time rope climbing and not enough paying attention to whatever it is that girls like. Judy rapidly faded from the picture after that. "You've got to check out a girl's mother," said my mother, "if you really want to know what she is going to be like." But Erik never did that with Judy's mother, so he would not have known how either one of them would react to a skunk on her porch. I heard later that her father did not think it was so good. Erik went back to rope climbing.

When a man has just experienced himself as a criminal, as I had, there is a lot to think about. I wandered in and out of classroom, back and forth across the wheat fields, more or less adrift. One day in class I heard Mrs. Post again: "Think, think, think," she said. "No," she said, "you there! Arnie! With your eyes closed! You're confusing sleep with thinking! Explore the difference!"

Post and sleep did not go together. When her face went all gray, nobody in our three grades even risked a twitch. It would take an hour or two, all through math and into geography, maybe, before a little wicked smile would creep up around her wrinkly, old mouth and she would let up.

After that, I tried as hard as I could to go by the rules. I tried not to do anything wrong. I started to be pretty hard to live with. Post could see it. I would want to enforce everything, make everybody obey, or do exactly what she said. One day she told a story.

"Once," she said, "there was a new married couple and they decided not to have any fights. So they made a rule. If the husband was in a bad mood when he came in from the field, he was to shift his pitchfork from his left to his right shoulder, and she would see him coming and know just what was the matter and be very nice, indeed. If the wife was in a bad mood, she was to tie a knot in her apron, and he would see the knot and tiptoe through the house, not disturbing her at all. Well, this rule worked for quite a while and they didn't have any fights. Then one day the husband came in with his pitchfork on his right shoulder and the wife had a knot in her apron, and what do you think happened?"

All six of us in the seventh grade sat there, not knowing what to say. The eighth and ninth graders must have heard the story before, but they knew better than to say a word, so they sat in their two rows, heads buried in their homework.

Nobody knew how to answer Post's question. So I said, "They fought."

"No," Post said. "They started laughing!" Her eyes lit up and her gray hair bobbed and her cheeks shone. "It takes more than rules to make a life!"

I wanted rules, so Post's story, which was supposed to be helpful, was very troubling. I wanted to know exactly what to do to be safe. I wanted to know exactly what to do to be good again. She wanted us to be flexible and to think. But thinking was dangerous, as far as I was concerned, and I was in a mood not to want any more surprises. I did not want any more dead men on my irrigation ditch. I did not want to be a cheater ever again.

Now it came a time in Arapahoe County when some things felt like death and some things felt like life. Winter snows laid down the grasses and the gray cottonwoods were stripped of leaves, dark and black against the January sky. Post said that rain, sun, seed, dirt, and little green shoots will come again, because they always do. She spoke of life.

But Louise, my friend, was picking up my blackness. Maybe there is something about a suicide that affects a whole area. She lived down the ditch just a little way from me, past the Big Bend. Or maybe it is that when one person at the table in the back of the room cheats, then the mood turns black for everyone. Or maybe Louise really did like me and wanted to show the black side for support. So she said to Mrs. Post: "No, not really. The spring does not always come; it's not that simple." Louise's family was into wheat, and Louise knew about failure. "Sometimes the rain doesn't fall. Sometimes there is more death and dying than we counted on. Sometimes the crop is blighted." Louise was probably the smartest person in our class. She said the spring comes, sure, but it takes more than spring. And then Eddie, who was still into pigs, got up his courage and said that sometimes people get sick without cause, and we all knew that he knew because his brother had polio and would never walk again. *Yeah,* said Ed, agreeing with Louise, *it takes more than spring.*

There was always talk during summers about who had just cut his alfalfa and who had left it lying down and vulnerable when the rains came, and how a man ought not to do that, as if some men could predict the weather and others couldn't. A farmer tried to read the reports, of course, and cut his hay by the predictions in the paper, or by the feel of the sky. He hoped that no rain would come because if the hay is already down, the drops take off the little green leaves and without leaves there is not much nourishment. We all knew this. *It takes more than rain.*

So I had this little league that consisted of me, Louise, and Eddie, people who knew that life is black and undependable. Then there was Darryl and his experience with Dexter. He knew too. On the other side were Mrs. Post, Mrs. Fredrickson, and my mother.

I was outside looking for rain clouds one day when I saw a hawk perched in a cottonwood above the Highline Canal, waiting. He was quiet and did not move except for his head, rotating his eyes this way and then that way, back and forth, looking, scanning. For a long time no birds came by, and then gradually they started flitting around distant branches and then closer, around the tree. The hawk held very still. The little birds didn't see him. Suddenly there was a flurry of desperate wings and a flash of gray through the leaves, and the hawk went down with a small bird in his talons, into the tall grass. I watched and felt sorry for the little bird. *What did it do,* I wondered, *to deserve to be the one that the hawk caught?* From all those birds around, how does just one get selected to be the one to die?

That night my father came to sit on the end of my bed. I told him about the hawk. I would never have the courage to talk about the suicide and cheating. Even to the best of men. Especially to the best of men. I thought I was supposed to be growing up and wanted to act like I would make him proud. So we talked about the hawk.

"You can't tell about death," he said. "It comes pretty unexpectedly sometimes. It wasn't the little bird's fault." He paused and wrinkled his nose and asked, as if he had wondered himself, "Death is not about fault, do you think?"

Nights when Don came to sit on the end of the bed had always been the best times of my life. I looked up at him now from under the covers and waited. "A lot of things are not about fault, though they may seem like it. Here in wheat country you can see the cycles. Seeing a long way, too, softens the certainty of things. Sometimes the grain fails because a man did not put the water on at the right time, and he should have. Sometimes it fails because there was no rain and none for miles around, and none even in the mountains, and it is not his fault at all. There are cycles. We don't always know what they are. We don't always know where we fit. But you can't tell a moral man just because he gets the rain. Sometimes a moral man does not get the rain and he is still a good person. Sometimes he makes a mistake and is still a good person."

I could feel my throat tighten and tears begin to fill my eyes, but it was dark and I thought he could not see. He went on. "Sometimes a bird gets caught and seems to be just unlucky, but I don't think you could say it was an immoral bird. What is unusual about America is that a man can have bad luck and start over and have a fair chance. That is why we have to be glad to live in this country." He slowed down to a soft stop and looked at me. "That's why our families, Thedia's and mine, went to the apple orchards of Oregon," he said. "That's why we came here. It will be true for you and all of us, even though the Barneses are not famous or rich or important. Every time we start over, there is a chance that one of you three might become something special." He looked softly at me and rubbed my hair. I couldn't take my eyes off him.

"You have been having a hard time," he said. "I know." He was quiet and didn't say anything for a little while. Then he said: "When you are outside, try seeing what your mother sees. When the wheat turns gold in the sunset and she shines in the glow of evening, or comes in with laughter in her eyes, you can see that she is enriched by wind and rain and grain and even the leaves flying. When you pay attention to those things, to the seasons, to the comings and goings, you begin to see a rhythm between death and life. Some things are pretty dependable. It is not that spring is always the solution, each time, but that the principle of spring is pretty reliable. There may be years without rain, or blight even, but there is always a mixture. Out on the ground there is death, but things renew. They always do, over and over. There is something fine about the natural order. Sometimes when it seems like one bird dies unfairly, remember that your mother knows that, too, and yet her face is always filled with awe." He leaned down and gave me a hug. I squeezed him tight and did not want to let go. He straightened and quietly left the room. I started to cry a little. But it was a cry of relief and warmth and joy.

That night, with him sitting there, I began to feel a thinning in the dark cloud of fear under which I had been living for many months. I began to think as I listened to his voice that some things happen that you can't predict, that I couldn't control, and that death was not all my fault. I did not have to be the one to pull the hose out of Mr. Rhea's car. I began to see that a lot of failures were not so important, including my not being good at math. I began to sleep without seeing the dead man's face in my dreams. I began to appreciate Fredrickson, Post, and my mother.

All through the summer months as a rule, our alfalfa patch was rich, dark green; our cottonwoods were an explosive yellow green bending along the canal. And underneath these great giant trunks were scattered prairie grass and buckbrush thickets, silver-gray after

October, or sometimes rust, or sometimes even copper, and then snow came and laid them all down. Most of the year, our world was under a shining blue sky, dotted here and there with thunderheads that looked to me like horses and lizards and, in the evening, like rolling balls of fire.

"Oh," my mother said one day, walking along the path on the way to the barn, "what a day!"

Savage's wheat field lay just beyond our alfalfa. On that afternoon it was glowing in a fading evening sun, the crop shimmering in July, shortly before harvest. From time to time, pushed by a breeze, the grain bent down and then as the wind lifted, the wheat heads drifted upright to catch and reflect the full glare of late, horizontal sun. A golden glow filled the evening air, spread out over the log barn and the cottonwoods, and covered my mother's face. "Oh, how lovely," she murmured.

Her world was filled with natural gold.

20.

The End of Curtis School

JUST WHEN I WAS ABOUT to become a person again, the officials of Arapahoe County determined that Curtis School was too small or too inefficient; the kind of worry that comes to minds of people who do not live near the land. So they closed our school. They sent us three and a half miles away to Littleton, which had several very urban disadvantages. It was a large city of five thousand people. The school building was white brick and not red. It had no bell tower. Where there should have been wheat fields, there were asphalt parking lots. There was not an irrigation ditch for swimming within at least two miles. Every class was in a different room and there was no Mrs. Post and no one in the world as gentle as Mrs. Fredrickson. There were at least five hundred kids milling around in the hallways. How could anyone be gentle? Only the best athletes got to play football and basketball, and although the girls were pretty—a factor of marginal importance—they mostly liked the athletes. They had very little regard for skinny little kids from the country in high-top black boots. I knew that all these things combined would have a bad effect on my character, and that the move to Littleton was therefore to be desperately resisted, so I told my mother so.

She said that when the officials make a decision, there is nothing we can do. There was none of the old Democrat fight in her. Gene Cervi would have resisted, but his kids went to Catholic schools so he was not involved. My mother just backed down and said, "I'll pack your lunch, same as usual." Maybe she and my father were worried about bigger things in the world. The Communists were closing down Berlin and there was a Cold War raging—way outside Arapahoe County—and maybe they thought a person should learn how to live in a big city as well as in the country so as to be prepared to be a Cold Warrior.

Before we transferred, three of us kids met on the ditch one day, talking about the world and what makes parents so distracted. I said I did not think the Communists would come to Littleton.

"Well, they could," Arnie Coughlin said. "They could. They are closing down Berlin. There are spies everywhere. They are leaving secret notes in pumpkins and they are giving away the atom bomb. Somebody ought to shoot one of those guys. Shoot Stalin. That would end it."

"They ain't goin' to shoot Stalin, and they ain't goin' to shoot nobody else," said Darryl.

"Well," Arnie grinned, "they ain't goin' to come here because Louise Elmore ain't pretty enough to take!"

He laughed hard. Louise was not around anywhere. Still, I was uncomfortable. I liked Louise. Sometimes a person is more pretty if there is more money around to get pretty with. I was sort of running this defense through my mind. But I did not say anything because I was not like Erik; I usually did not say the truth just because it was there. Anyway, we were talking about Communists.

So the world was falling apart outside, Arnie thought we were in danger, and Darryl and I didn't know. I left Curtis just before the ninth grade, just before I could become king of the mountain. Instead, Littleton's ninth grade was the lowest in the new school and I was on the bottom again. We went from talking about alfalfa and County Fair to motor oil, pool halls, and parties on Saturday night. I was not naive. I knew about Saturday nights. I had had a whiff of parties in the dark of people's living rooms, lights off, and boys and girls scraggled up in knots on the couch. I was scared.

Frank had a 1930 Dodge that he had painted bright blue with white wooden wheel spokes. He was not an athlete, particularly, because he was still gangly and not real fast on his feet, but he had made a splash in Littleton with that Dodge. He drove us to the new school. On cold days he drove with his head out the window because the old Dodge wheezed steam so bad it looked like a locomotive and there was no vision out the windshield. This was hard on his ears, and by the time we got to school his mouth was so frozen he could not talk. Maybe this explains why he was good at math because no talking is needed in that subject. Frank put a bucket of water in the Dodge's trunk in the mornings to be used for the radiator on the afternoon drive home. I guess the old Dodge never went fast enough to spill the water, and I don't know why the bucket didn't freeze back there in the trunk all during the day, but that is what he did.

One night, after one of Littleton High's Friday night football games, somebody's mother drove some of us kids home. The vehicle was loaded with youngsters. "Tell me where to go," she said, looking at me. She was sort of a city lady.

"Straight up here," I said. Then I said, "Right here will be fine, thank you."

"Here?" she asked. We were along an empty stretch of road about a quarter mile from any trees. The lady stopped the car, but there was no house anywhere. The woman was very well mannered and did not say anything.

"Yes," I said, opening the door and stepping out into the dark alfalfa. "Goodnight." I ran across the gravel road and trotted out into the middle of an empty hay field. I dropped down into the alfalfa and lay flat on my belly, hiding, motionless. The driver lady paused a long time on the road and finally drove away. I got up and walked home, like Oliver Twist, tap-dancing across the fields, humming. I was at home out there. I was in my territory, in alfalfa, in the cool air of night, sure of everything around me, far more secure and happy than ever I was on a sidewalk in town. I was showing off for those city kids and the lady driver whom I never saw again. But I didn't tell my father about this at all, ever, or my mother, for a very long time, because in general they disapproved of people pretending to be something they were not. They would especially not think it was good to pretend to be poor and without a real house. They thought that in general it was better to pretend to be smart. And they would not have thought that this was a very good way to make new friends. Still, I had my little protest and nobody could doubt that I was a real country boy after that. I was the boy who lived in a hole in the middle of an alfalfa field.

We tried to think of a way to stay connected to old Mrs. Post. She needed friends, too, now that we were gone. The principal of Littleton High was a man named Mr. Ervin. On Halloween we went to see him to put some potato spuds in the exhaust pipe of his car. It was another of those criminal tendencies brought to the city by boys from the country. Mr. Ervin emerged on the porch of his house just as we were scouting out the territory. "Oh, hello!" We were very nice. He was, as it turned out, plastering his living-room walls that night. Somehow the subject of Mrs. Post came up. Somehow it also came up to make her a dish of hot fudge from Mr. Ervin's plaster. He got out a tin and mixed plaster and chocolate and cut it all into squares. In about ten minutes the whole mixture set up like a sweet rock. We drove out to find Post.

"Why, boys, how nice of you," she smiled, "how very thoughtful." We gave her the plaster brownies. "For you," Frank said innocently. She said, "For me? For pity sakes! Why, boys, you must have a seat and have some of these with me." We sat down as if we might take some because a person had to be a little bit crafty with Post. But finally we said no, we had had quite a lot of Halloween candy already, thank you, and would not like any brownies just now. After we had sat quietly squirming for about ten minutes, I started to feel pretty bad. Post wore false teeth and she was probably going to break her teeth and not be able to eat. We would be in for another thrashing.

Post just kept talking and talking like it was Sunday night at the teahouse, and it seemed like there were no end of interesting things to discuss. "Did you know," she asked, watching the three farm-boy prisoners on her couch wiggle, "that this year we are probably not going to have the rain we did last year?" She smiled like a little fragile angel woman who was torturing criminals. "I believe the County Fair will be very nice next year, too," she said. Post never talked about the Fair, and especially not a year in advance. "Why, boys," she said, "are you hungry yet? Would you like some fudge now?" We declined again, politely. "Well, then," she said, "boys, thank you for your thoughtfulness in visiting an old lady on this lovely occasion," and ushered us to the door.

That was the last connection we had with Curtis School.

21.

World Training

SINCE WE WERE ALREADY on the slippery slope toward urban decadence, my mother decided to take us to California to show us the world. There were things out there that were even way more advanced than Littleton. Grandmother Schellenberg still lived there in the same house she had when my father and mother decided to get married. There was elegance out there. There was the Sewall history. There was Grandmother Schellenberg's chapel and Grandmother Barnes's mystical writing, her channeling of the ancients. If we thought Littleton was sophisticated, we had another think coming.

One of the things I learned right away was that in California women talk a lot. In Grandmother Schellenberg's kitchen my mother and her two sisters, Betsy and Mary, discussed the whole world, the Cold War, the First War, the Second War, and the politics of 1896 when Grandmother's grandfather, Frank Sewall, ran for vice president of the United States. They talked about

Grandmother Schellenberg's opera, never quite finished, and about her stint as postmistress of Palos Verdes Estates. She must have been the most exciting postmistress in the history of the postal service. From the way she described her life, the women at the post office talked about painting and music, the Colonial Ball, ants in the honey, Democrats, and progress. They talked about all of it, all of the time, all together, and Grandmother brought all the news back to her kitchen.

My father would escape to the living room and read by the fire. Erik and Frank and I would sneak across the street onto the golf course and look for lost golf balls in the high grass under the eucalyptus trees. I had never seen eucalyptus trees before. They were to Palos Verdes and my grandmother's house the same as cottonwoods were to us, the signature of the landscape. When we three boys got back with an armload of recovered golf balls, somebody would say, "How nice, boys," but they would plunge on forward with the latest word on the reforms in the Swedenborgian church. They seemed like they were rushing to get every problem in the world solved before dinner.

"Which one of these sweet boys will set the crystal and fill the glasses for dinner?" asked Grandmother.

"Craig will," said Erik, "he's sweet."

Violence immediately erupted. I landed a hard right fist to Erik's shoulder. "Boys!" shouted my mother. "Boys!" Whereupon Erik and I were summarily banished outside "to find something constructive to do" and Frank, scowling, had to pour the water.

"Hey, wait a second!" he said.

"He's the sweetest," I said.

"Out!" said my mother.

Erik and I shuffled into the garden. "Worked," he said.

It was a long way from Coventry Hall, Maine, where Grandmother Schellenberg spent her summers as a child in the 1890s, to Arapahoe County. Grandmother was doing her best to bridge the gap. She told us to set the table with her finest silver and finest dishes, and we drank only bottled water. She put her mashed potatoes in silver covered dishes and her carrots on a silver platter, and her roast lamb was juicy and hot as if it was from France.

"Will somebody please play the piano after dinner?" she pleaded, and then explained to us boys, "I've had music around me all my life." She paused. "Until I was married."

"That," said my Aunt Betsy dryly, "was up until fifty years ago. You've had some life since then, Mother!"

The ancients from Coventry Hall hung in great portraits on Grandmother's staircase and glowered at small boys who slid down the banister. "That old battle-ax was your ancestor, boys," said Grandmother, laughing. "Doesn't she look like she has a stomach-ache!?"

"Mother!" said Betsy, but everybody laughed. The old battle-ax had a high white collar and a little white cap on her curly head and filled the stairwell with her glower. It seemed right, though, that she should hang in a house with wide oak floors, a grand fireplace, blue handblown Mexican glasses, and silver trays.

Grandmother, in fact, did not have much money. But she remembered elegance from those far-off early days before she was married, before the lumber mill burned down, when she was a child traveling with her cosmopolitan father in Europe, when her father was a well-known Swedenborgian minister prominent in Washington, D.C. She loved to speak of things delicate, frilly lace and purples in stained glass. She loved the drama of politics. She had painted watercolors in narrow lanes in Tuscany and took us boys to the beach to watch the colors when the waves crashed. Things with her were seldom "good." They were "grand." If she said only "That's good," we looked around to see what was wrong.

Not only my mother's mother but also my father's was here. She lived in Pasadena, two hours' drive away. "Mom" had a special talent that was just about as good as writing opera. She could put her pen to paper and write words dictated to her by Leonardo da Vinci and Molière. She called these sessions "automatic writing" and had published books about conversations with Voltaire and Henry James and her own father. Mom was scholarly and quiet, the opposite of Grandmother Schellenberg, but she communicated with the ancients, which was in itself "very grand."

My own mother was very uncertain about the automatic writing with dead people; talking to Molière made her nervous, but there was nothing to do about it. Mom was as humble and as truthful as any seamstress and probably the smartest and most widely read person in the room, my father included. So she was California, too, quietly sitting by the fire during word games, amused at all the chatter, laughing quietly, proud of her Donald.

California was gas stations and oil well derricks and more asphalt than in a hundred Littleton High School parking lots. It was the ocean and blue forever. Grandmother Schellenberg had decided before the end of the war to build a Swedenborgian chapel for wayfarers, people who wandered along the California coast and liked to stop and look out over the ocean and pray. "With grand trees inside and outside, with plants blooming along the altar, with the great blue sea stretching away so far that only God is greater!" she exclaimed to her family around the dining-room table. We three boys said that when she was talking like that, she "was having freight trains." *Huff, puff, puff.* But we loved it. She was the most enthusiastic person in the room, always. Any room, anywhere.

Sometimes Grandmother's four deaf sisters came to join us at the table. They wore black only, head to toe, and seemed always to be in mourning about one thing or another. They cut out paper dolls "for the little boys" who did not think they were quite that little, and these aunts shouted instructions or questions more or less all at once. They could not hear the difference between "sea" and "tea" and would put coats on just when we were sitting down, or would sit down looking for sugar and cream just when we were bundling up for the car. Long ago when they were young girls before the turn of the twentieth century, the five sisters had walked the country lanes of Italy together, painting watercolors of chapels and the Italian seacoast. The old aunts were now the nearest living equivalent to Mom's dead writing companions, but since they were nearly stone-deaf, speaking to them was harder than speaking to the dead. All Mom had to do was pick up a pen and tune in Molière. The aunts did not wear hearing aids for they didn't think they were really deaf. They preferred to shout loudly, at table, for the salt, or to sit meekly pretending to understand, smoothing down their black dresses with crumpled old fingers.

My mother took us to California to meet the world. We dug for crabs in the sand, compared wheat fields with the blue ocean, and crawled, dripping wet and cold, back up the hill on a December afternoon when Grandmother put real candles on her Christmas tree and we boys vied to be the ones to light the tree and then blow the candles out when we left the room. When dinner was over, she assembled us around the fireplace and reminded us all again that she had had music around her all her life, coercing my mother to play Christmas carols, or my father to play "Für Elise." Then we circled and played word games, making stories that each person contributed to, every word in the story beginning with the same letter. Or she would ask Don to read a poem, or ask one of her many guests to explain what life was really like, these days, in Washington, D.C.

Like a person learning two languages, I learned Grandmother-speak and Arapahoe County–speak, and the two never mixed. When I went back to Littleton, I never breathed a word of California, or Grandmother's house, the oak floors, the fine blue glasses, the opera and the poems, the speaking with Molière. Grandmother tried to join the two worlds. But she was on a different stage. It was not a stage of show only, or pomp, or glamour to impress the world. She loved conversation naturally, like a raven loves to fly, and the color purple, sunsets, and serenades.

I didn't think much of California's gas stations and asphalt. But Mrs. Fredrickson had told us in the fifth grade about Odysseus on the wine-dark sea, about voyages of discovery and adventure. "Everyone moves on," she had said. From Grandmother's second-floor window we could look out over the eucalyptus that lay below her house and in the far distance glimpse this sea stretching away forever.

On the last night, we went down by the ocean to have a beach cookout with hot dogs and cheese and a campfire. My father and mother and her two sisters, Betsy and Mary, sang cowboy songs by the whispering waves. The air was salty and the wind warm. Driftwood crackled in the flames and Aunt Mary taught us to sing "Skyball Paint" and Don and the two sisters leaned together and looked out to the heaving sea singing, "There's a long, long trail a-winding . . . into the land of my dreams. . . ."

"Good-bye," said Mom, she hugged my father as we prepared to drive home the next morning. "Keep an eye out," she breathed, "what with everything going on in Berlin and Greece and Turkey, even Taiwan; keep an eye out." He hugged her and looked at her seriously because Mom so seldom gave advice.

"We're all together," he said, "we're all right."

"For now," she said, hugging him again.

"Can you keep them on the farm, now?" Grandmother Schellenberg emerged from the house, bubbly.

"Craig has to sit in the middle because he's the sweetest," said Erik.

"Noo!"

"In," said my father. The old people were a little choked up. Not me. My Littleton mind had been pried open and stuffed richer than turkey dressing at Thanksgiving. Grandmother was the closest thing to Henry V that I had ever met: exuberant, full of enthusiasm, and yet, somehow, against all the odds, both carried away and still good.

"I don't know," said my mother, "we'll have to see."

22.

The Second Leaving

I LEARNED ABOUT FALLING OFF HORSES all by myself and about getting back up on a horse from Erik. I learned about saving money from Frank. I learned about gold from my mother, who had learned about purple and blue Mexican glass from her mother. I learned about fighting from Arnie Coughlin and about death from Carlos Rhea. I learned about gentleness and square corners from my father. Altogether, that is about enough to grow up. If a man can tell what is gold, can fight and be gentle, and can make a square corner, how much more is there?

"Well," my father said, "you ought to think about that fighting."

"Okay. So fighting is a last resort."

"More like failure, really."

"Okay. Yeah, you're right. That's good because I am scared mostly, and I won't make much of a fighter.

"You're all right," he said, "but when it comes to blows, you miss your chance at civilization." I was supposed to know by then that while the ancients had made war, Americans were to be pioneers in making peace, learning how to do the "civil" part of civilization. That was what all those bedside talks had been about.

"Okay," I said, like I was not listening. But the truth is I was listening and the search for the "civil" in civilization had become Don's internal command, branded in my brain.

I didn't know it, but the training period was almost over. I had soil in my hair and wind in my eyes but I was about to get blown out of there and this time not because of any little thing like a suicide or my own petty moral character. I was about to get hefted by history.

"Reds Attack!" was the headline in *The Denver Post*, June 20, 1950. I thought of the Cincinnati Reds blasting the Brooklyn Dodgers. My hero, Ralph Branca, got blasted off the mound. Dodgers lose again. But that was not these Reds. These were other Reds, and they were headed down the peninsula of Korea, hell-bent for conquest.

Within two weeks the Truman government was beefing up Allied forces in Europe and a phone call brought an end to my life in Arapahoe County.

My mother answered the phone. I was hanging upside down on the couch, marking time. Morning feeding was done, the day was quiet. It was warm, the sound of grasshopper wings carried on a dry plains breeze. No one had called for Colonel Barnes since the end of the second war. I watched my mother with my feet dangling above me. I saw her face go pale and heard her cheerful voice become hard. She said, *No, the Colonel is not here, but he can be reached at the office.* She gave the number. She hung up and sat down, quiet or numb. The call was from the Pentagon. Colonel Barnes had been a camouflage officer in World War II, and was needed in England to be part of a reinforced defense for Western Europe. It was about twelve noon on a Saturday. On Monday, he had packed and was gone.

The Communists were attacking Korea, but they had been blustering in Europe for years. Stalin had closed down Berlin and set off their own atomic bomb, and his allies had closed Poland, Hungary, and Czechoslovakia and threatened Greece. Harry Truman had defended Greece, drawn a line in the sand, and it had worked. Then, for years, the two Great Powers were eyeball to eyeball, waiting for one another to blink. When the North Koreans launched an invasion in the Orient in 1950, Western defenses tightened all over the world, waiting for the next assault. Don had been an officer in World War II, an engineer hiding airfields and bases from German airpower. Now something like that was needed in England, and when the whistle blew they called him back. We knew all this history because even after the war my mother never stopped listening to the radio. This story had been in our living room, night after night, from 1948 on.

When the phone call came that June afternoon we did not know it, but we had listened for the last time to Don reading aloud from the big chair about *Black Bartleme's Treasure*; we had heard from him the last Luke Short western. His favorite had always been Sherlock Holmes. He had read Holmes to us when all his world was right, for pure pleasure, when mystery was bloodless intrigue and efficient intelligence reigned. But now our life in Arapahoe County began to wind down. Over the course of the next months, after the phone call, we would pluck our last chicken at killing time and carry water in a bucket for the '30 Dodge for the last time.

To me, to have received a personal call from the Pentagon, from an officer who had known him during the Second World War, to be remembered, to be needed, was something of an honor. I thought somebody must think my father was awfully smart. It was not a shock to think that he was being called to do some heroic deed in defense of the Western world. It was what we had prepared for, by reading Shakespeare and studying Latin and the great myths. It was in the nature of being high-minded, which he encouraged in all that he did. So there was no question of his turning down the call or not going.

My mother had planned, on that Saturday before the call came, that we would go to the evening ballet at Red Rocks Amphitheater. We went ahead with the plan. Ballet was part of her effort to bring us in touch with what Grandmother Schellenberg would have loved and she would not give it up for some small reason. Or perhaps it had become all the more important that we be together because he would soon again be gone. We sat in the open amphitheater in the high mountains, great cliffs reaching up to the open sky on both sides. Emotionally we were numb, in shock. There was irony in watching the Ballet Russe, with its great Russian ballerina, in Colorado, and in Don having to leave to defend our world against a Russian government. I sat there under the stars listening to Tchaikovsky's music, watching twirls and leaps on the stage, wind in my hair, with several thousand people in the audience. I thought that probably Don was the only person in that whole packed amphitheater to receive a call that day from the Pentagon, saying *Come back to work, we need you, your country needs you.* After a while, I leaned over to him with tears in my eyes and said, "You must be the smartest man in all of Red Rocks." He smiled, but his mind and heart and attention were already gone.

23.

This Is It, Then

"WELL, TRAVEL IS BROADENING," said my mother hope-fully, and when, after some months, Don did not come back, we went together to join him in England. Frank by now was in Princeton, where my mother had said all along he should go because her father had gone there. Frank was launched, except that in his letters he said he was studying until two or three every morning, which worried my mother some, and me a lot. I did not like the prospect of ever having to do that, and college certainly was part of her family plan. Erik was off that fall to Colorado A&M to study veterinary medicine, a stop, he thought, on the road to owning a ranch. He would be satisfied with any ranch, anywhere. That left only one boy at home, me. In September 1951, my mother and I boarded a train at Union Station in the oldest part of Denver, rolled east for Chicago and on to New Jersey, where we boarded a troop ship for the six-day ocean passage to England.

During the months before we left, one by one, I gave away or sold all the foundations of my rural life.

Chickens I gave to the Liggetts, sheep I left with Hecky Heckendorf in Littleton, in hopes that I would be back soon. The dogs, including Stormy, we gave to someone whom I had never known. Stormy, the black and white mostly English setter I had seen born in a box in the basement of the white house and had raised from the first hour of his life. I had wrestled with him in every buckbrush thicket along the canal, chased magpies with him, taken him for long rides on Chita to the far corners of the prairie. Stormy had been a regular companion perhaps because, unlike any older brother, he was always eager to waste time wandering the fields, hunting down squirrels, inspecting nests at swallows' bridge, whenever and wherever I had the urge, and he never asked me to fix fence. Now I gave Stormy away to someone nameless. I wondered if the North Koreans knew what they were doing, forcing me to pull life up by the roots and give it away to strangers. A gray cold mood settled over my summer.

A thread of continuity in our young people's church group had been square dancing. The last summer, we danced two or three times a week, on our lawn under the cottonwoods (the one we had dug by hand because Smoky the plow horse broke the plow), on Cody Fletcher's lawn or Darlene's lawn over on the other side of Belleview, in the streets at Central City's music festival up in the mining country, at the Red Rocks Amphitheater in the mountains, under the stars. From Cody and Darlene in their bright, flowery full dresses, I learned wide-eyed abandon and saw bubbly laughter that lit the stars. Here was something exquisite, clean, and vivacious that stirred a new happiness and also some dark anguish that I had not yet experienced.

The minister's son, Dave Chandler, played banjo and sang of his cross-eyed, snaggle-toothed sweetheart or of Dan Tucker's mother-in-law, or of every poor minstrel's sad and sorry life. He sang with wrinkled-nose whimsy and wry laughter that brought us crowding around his knee, chortling and teasing about the rich and the old and the unfortunate few who could not be like us, the children of the West. We square-danced on the lawn under great spreading cottonwoods with a Victrola plugged into a long line through the window inside the nearest house, or we danced to live callers. We danced for the joy of being young and free. In the square dancing I found some antidote for my permanent status as a stranger, some acceptable bridge between being a country boy and the stirring of new passions.

Then, after the farewells, the pictures, the promises, my mother and I were on our way to England. From Littleton's five thousand to London's multiple millions. It seemed clear to me as I sat on the silver train heading east across Colorado, nose to the window watching wheat fields fall away and pass behind, that I would never again square-dance under the stars, or see Stormy loping through tall grass quartering for pheasants. This was, of course, true. I never did.

In London, it rained and rained. We sat around a coal fire to keep warm. We were good at this. We were fire people. The British seemed not to have discovered central heating, but we had had our own bouts in the blizzards. I sank into a kind of black depression. Dark

London was a world without hope. I was led by my mother to castles to learn English history. I waited for each weekend when we would go search out some Technicolor Western at a local cinema. I told everybody who would listen that those horses in the mountains, that prairie, that toughness of the men they saw in the movies, was the country I came from. "Country" as in pure, rough, and wide open. I was from there, I said. We saw *Broken Arrow* and *Bend in the River* with Jimmy Stewart, my kind of man, indirect and soft-spoken but with grim grit when the arrows of death were honing in. I said I was from Indian country, too, only a few years after what you see there on the screen. I had a coonskin cap that I had brought with me from Littleton, and I wore it on the streets of London, in Piccadilly and Trafalgar Square. *I am,* I said, *a western man.* We saw a rerun of *Gone with the Wind,* which was not technically a Western but had a decent amount of color and suffering to be a good advertisement for the heroic rural life.

English boys my age wore short pants. I would not do that and at first stayed in Levi's. Then I was fitted for a Harris tweed sport coat and black slacks, which made my mother's eyes sparkle because the new tweed was of such fine quality. One awful November day, the tailor wrapped me in my new coat and I looked at myself in the mirror. Just then the bells of an old stone church down the street began to ring, tolling some death or other. *Mine,* I thought. On a radio Nat King Cole was singing "Too Young" and I said to myself, "You got that right."

The coat was intensely scratchy but good enough for warmth, I conceded. It became my protection through a freezing and drizzly winter when I was cold all the way to the heart. Never in all the history of Arapahoe County had there been as much fog as lay in a single afternoon on Baker Street in London. The tweed coat, I supposed, was a mark of my mother's civilization in an otherwise uncivilized, crowded, and unfeeling world, and it was, after all, good to see her eyes sparkle.

At first, there was no school to prepare a man for an American college. Not finding anything the equivalent of Littleton High, I rode the Tube every day through fog, smog, and crowds to what the English called a "tutor school," where I could be tutored for college as if I had failed in normal school and had to try again. *It was fitting*, I thought, *for a person who had failed miserably to keep himself in Arapahoe County*. This cost, too, the North Koreans must have overlooked when they invaded South Korea.

Where before I had learned the trails of squirrels and rabbits beneath the brush along the Highline Canal, now I learned the underground trails of the London Tube and daily maneuvered through crowds of commuters for an hour and a half all the way from Ruislip Manor, Baker Street, Paddington Station, and finally up into the world of pale light at Warwick Avenue. Here I ascended to sidewalks before rows of darkly solemn, Victorian, five-story dwellings, each connected to the next; airless, tight, squeezed together during an early industrial age when my fields in Arapahoe County had been peopled primarily by pheasants and Indians.

From the outside, these homes appeared as if they might be withered middle-class castles. Inside, they were gloomy with heavy maroon velvet curtains, dusky-paned windows, dark stairs. A schoolboy had to feel his way up these stairs led by a polished oaken railing past the headmaster's forbidden lodgings, past his kitchen, past his mysterious and often-mentioned sickly wife. Up and around we groped, three flights to enter a dark room directly opposite the stairwell. When I arrived early enough, I could select a chair near the coal fire. But each morning I had an hour-and-a-half Tube ride and I usually ended up a serious distance from the heat, near the end of a green study table where students were solemnly tutored in everything from Caesar to Chaucer, but no subject much nearer in time than the sixteenth century.

This end of the green table was, unfortunately, directly beside a perpetually open window. The English thought the draft was healthy. Or they thought that schoolboys should be cold to improve their attitudes. Or they thought that they were in training for the next war. I don't know. The fire burned at one end of the room and the casement window was open at the other. On the frontier where I was from, I said, a person knew to close the door, to save firewood and keep wolves out. The English had no position on wolves. I froze. Latin, I soon found out, does not stick to iced brain cells.

There was no comparison, of course, between this life and the rural life of Arapahoe County. A boy could tell that to fit in he had to be remade from the ground up, from the clothes he wore to the subjects he talked about. The British did not know to keep the wolves out and did not know the difference between a grand-champion chicken and an ordinary chicken, or a black ant and a piss ant, skills upon which I had made a life. They were into kings, trumpets, and the Battle of Britain, "subjects," my mother said hopefully, "that once you loved, don't you remember?"

I could not remember that far back. The only remnant of civilization we had in Colorado as old as their Norman castles was the Anasazi ruins at Mesa Verde. Every single public building in London had to predate the Arapahoe County Courthouse. Graffiti scattered on the walls of bombed-out London said, "Yank, go home!" and I was more than willing, not because I did not like these people or because they were not decent, but because I did not know how to talk, how to be, and, more than anything, I wanted to be somewhere where I could be understood. In literature class there was an assignment to read Ralph Waldo Emerson, who told me, personally, that to be great was to be misunderstood. *Yes,* I said.

After a year, I fell desperately in love with a sixteen-year-old with the improbable name of Snooky, also an exile from America. Her name was unusual but her heart was big, and there was a rumor that we kissed, proving the value of the Harris tweed sport coat.

Then our family moved again, almost immediately, demonstrating that love is a temporary and overrated solution to anything. This time we went to Athens, Greece. There, the sun shone and the Parthenon gleamed in the moonlight and Mrs. Fredrickson's myths rallied around to give me orientation. We drove to Marathon and Delphi and Sparta. We swam in the

Aegean, and slowly in these warm waters my soul began to unfold somewhat, as it had not done since leaving Littleton. Maybe it was the sunshine.

I was no longer a cowboy or a trainee Indian. I was no longer a London schoolboy. In fact, I was no longer anything that fit any package. I had been robbed, and freed, of labels. This is not what I had hoped for. It had always seemed okay to me to be a cowboy or a rancher.

"Well," said Don, "it's not as if we had some plan to come here. We did not make this happen of our own intention. But you are becoming a citizen of the whole, international world scene." It was 1953. He had been able to leave the military as the Korean War turned a corner and start a new career as an engineer to do water work, dams, and construction from Saudi Arabia to Turkey. The world was opening before him, too.

For me, in Greece, wishing for something to hang on to, I once again chose a girl. Falling in love seemed the best thing a reasonable person could do in the circumstances. I did that now a second time, with the same result. Her name was Susan and we swam in the Aegean and admired temples greatly. We met under the Acropolis, held hands under a full moon beside the Parthenon, and believed we shared the love of the ages. She led me by the hand across the plains of Marathon and we sat under olive trees and talked of being older. I no longer had any thought that Erik's solution of learning to rope climb was better than this. The sea waters were warm and sparkling clear, and here, with Mrs. Fredrickson's Odysseus, I fell in love with the wine-dark sea. Then, as in the myths, Susan's father moved, the golden girl left, and I left. My father was transferred to build dams and roads in Rangoon, Burma; again, a new place.

In Rangoon, one September night in 1953, an important conversation occurred.

I was outside. A gentle, tropical breeze stirred the banyan leaves above my head. I was seventeen, about to leave for Switzerland to complete the last year of high school. I had spent that summer in the jungles of upper Burma, traveling by train and bus under a darkly forested canopy, winding from one thatched village to the next. By now I was so distant from Arapahoe County that I was afraid to go back, afraid to be more strange there than I had been when I first landed in London. I was no longer a country boy. I was now some sort of hybrid and confident that I could make it in Europe on my own, but not confident that I would know what to say or how to be if I went back to farm country, to Arapahoe County.

Where three years earlier, I had had to be pried out of Littleton, now I was uncertain that I could fit back in. I did not know if I could talk Littleton. In London, I had picked up a British accent. That was okay in Athens and Rangoon. It would be ridiculous in Littleton. And I had changed in what I liked. I had found the haunts of kings. I had become thoroughly affected by the cathedrals of London, the white temples of Greece, the golden pagodas of Rangoon. Since I had never been able to talk about Grandmother Schellenberg's purple stained glass and silver in Littleton, I said to myself self-consciously, I won't know what to talk about at home. I don't really have a home. *You get the world,* my father said, *but you lose the sweet smell of home.*

We therefore chose together, my parents and I, that I would return to Europe, a Swiss boarding school, for the last year.

Rangoon, outside at night in summer, was eerily noisy. Frogs croaked on the dark edge of a smooth, black lake, big-winged insects clattered in the heavy canopy above me, geckoes chuckled inside on the painted walls of the bungalow in which we lived. One cannot escape these sounds on any tropical summer night. All the blackness was alive and noisy. My father was working as an engineer in yet another country and we had come to join him as much for that, he said with whimsy and a sparkle in his eye, as for any intention to wreck my last, most perfect love.

The way to stop the spread of communism in Southeast Asia, America was convinced, was to build economies and create income, concrete, roads, schools, and lumber mills where before under the British Empire there had only been exploitation. *Saving the world requires sacrifices,* he said; *moving on is a constant, is built in.* That is why we were there. But now I was moving on, grown old enough to fend on my own, to leave with his blessing.

I stood on the black shore of a lake called Inle and watched long rays of yellow light play across the water from a canteen somewhere on the other side. In a bar over there someone was playing a record. The voice sang: "Ten thousand miles away from home . . . and it will be the death of me. . . ."

I had been a Littleton, Colorado, farm boy and was no more. Quickly in succession, I had been a Londoner, a student of Greece, and now I was headed back to learn French and German, to prepare somehow for life beyond pigs and chickens and County Fair. Frangipani and orchid smells lay hot on the grass and above our heads insects and bats flew in and out of the glow from the bungalow windows. I shifted from foot to foot, shyly confident at last but awestruck by the coming separation.

The father of fathers stood beside me, quietly. We watched the live jungle night, heard it, were taken in by the enormity of the coming parting, said nothing, but watched the light dance on dark water.

Soon, perhaps as soon as the next flight from Rangoon to Calcutta, I would be gone. "When you get off in Zurich," he said quietly at last, "take the bus from the airport directly to the train station. German for train is 'Zug.' There should be a train direct from Zurich to St. Gallen and you will probably not have to change. You will be able to read 'St. Gallen' because it is the same in English. Get off there. Somebody from the school may meet you at the station. If not, well, perhaps someone at the ticket counter or a newsstand will speak English and give you directions. You have the name of the school in your billfold?" I nodded. "If it is not too late at night, you should make it. You have had a lot of experience in railway stations and sleeping on benches, if it comes to that."

"Yes," I said, quietly, as a man would say it. I was seventeen. It was true, after three years in Europe, I had had a lot of experience in railway stations.

I ventured then to say what I would like to become, some day, in the world I was stepping out into. "I would like to write," I said. My heart was full. "I would like to be able to describe the great Irawaddy River in flood the way I saw it in the Burma hill country this summer: golden in the sunset, everywhere golden, the world afloat in orange gold. I remember," I said, "that just then, when I saw it like that, like a huge copper sheet spread across the face of the earth, a tiny jungle boatman cut a single dark line across the surface, carving a thin human flaw. There was an awesome power, like a great copper stream—a mile wide—floating past, cut by that thin, dark line, and beyond, on the other side, the sun's glow abruptly stopped at the edge of an endless, black impenetrable jungle." All through this I had been struggling for words to match the awesome power of a scene experienced one afternoon earlier that summer. I had been alone that day and now wanted to tell him of it.

My father listened quietly. I went on: "I think about the Arapahoe County cottonwoods still, too, green and swaying in a storm, and about the wheat come full and golden. Gold everywhere, I guess. I wish I could describe it. I think about timothy grass turning purple and feathery in the fall, the smell of bark and dry grass in November, magpies on a wintering wind, and even," I looked him in the eyes, "about the smell of dust one day when I stood with you in the barn." I paused. "I want to learn to be a writer. That is where my heart is."

Finally, I said, "I wish you could have a chance to read it." My throat tightened and I stopped, unable to go on.

"You do pretty well," he said, "just talking it."

If someone knew us and was listening, he or she would have known that this short sentence from him was support and hope and love and caution, all mixed together. He did not intend to understate his praise, it was just that we talked in measured ways, still, in a sort of code of the wheat country. There was still Arapahoe County in us. "You already do speak well," he said. Praise and caution.

Then the caution took over. "Come to think of it, I wanted to be a writer once myself. But it is important to be practical. There is the matter of earning a living. It is hard for writers. It is possible to get swallowed by the feeling thing. You have to be careful." Years before, his father had been carried away. He simply wandered away and never came back. Being carried away was a danger for a man. I knew this from that one conversation, those long years ago, the only time we had ever talked of his father. I accepted his caution as the ground accepts rain.

Don was not sure that the life of a writer could be a life of goodness, of consideration and thoughtfulness. He thought that life for any person who had been abundantly given to should be one of giving back. He was not sure a writer could do that without being consumed by self-pity or indulgence. He was not sure where the raw emotional life could take a man. He would want his son to be careful.

That night I knew, if Don was not sure, that I could not be sure either. I knew that from that moment. The writing life would not be mine. The music from the canteen stopped and no longer came across the water. A warm wind lifted my thin tropical shirt.

"Keep your eye out for what is fine, old man," he said, hugging me a long moment. It was to be the last time we would live in the same house, he and I, a third and final leaving, only this time it was the boy who was going away for a long time.

I peered into the gloomy night for signs of what was to come.

"This is it, then," he said. He put a hand on my head and ruffled my hair. Then he went inside.

Postlude

Frank was admitted to Princeton University the year the Korean War began. He went on to get a doctorate at Stanford University and became a professor of electrical engineering and chairman of his department at the University of Colorado, where he is still teaching. He consults for laboratories all over the country and since 1991 has worked extensively to create opportunities in Western science for researchers from the former Soviet Union. He has nurtured hundreds of Boulder students into lives of science and engineering. In 1997 he was named a Distinguished Professor by the trustees of the university, an honor bestowed upon fewer than twenty people in the history of the university. In 2001 he was elected to the National Academy of Engineering, the highest honor in his field.

In 1951 Erik enrolled at Colorado A&M from which he went on to become a veterinarian. He practiced veterinary medicine and was a set net fisherman in Alaska and on the Bering Sea. When the fish were not running, he was a bush pilot, mountain climber, explorer for gold in Panama, and devoted husband and father. In the late 1980s he fulfilled the dream that began with the Catch-It-Calf contest at the Arapahoe County Fair. He bought a thousand-acre cattle ranch that lies beyond the range of any telephone amidst saguaro cactus and rocks in wildest Arizona. Today, he can step into a round corral of newly captured mustangs and, from thirty feet, pick one out, play a mix between cougar and human being—back up and go forward in a dance—and lead a wild mustang to walk out of the pack all the way up to take the halter.

My mother was named Mother of the Year in 1951 by the *Littleton Independent*. It was an honor she accepted with great modesty. The award was an unsolicited confirmation that all she had set out to do—holding the family together with those Saturday hikes in the high country through the war years, settling her family on the barren prairie through County Fair time and broken-ribs time—was somehow not easy and had been well done. The recognition signaled that she, too, had been part of the great American story, her values and those of the community sang together. After Littleton, she and Don lived in London, Athens, Rangoon, Addis Ababa, and Washington, D.C., while he did engineering and she was forever engaged in the community, raising money for children, enjoying conversation in the evenings, eager for the next news. In the late 1960s they retired and returned to live again in Littleton, in the white house by the irrigation ditch under the cottonwoods. Of all the places that my mother had lived, none had ever been more home to her, or more imprinted on her, than Colorado during those five years between the end of one war and the beginning of the next. She knew how to make people comfortable at her table anywhere. She was most comfortable herself, however, with the high mountains out her windows to the west and the plains falling away to the east.

Don died in 1990. The family gathered in the living room of the white house where the saplings my mother had planted in 1946 had become tall maples, ash, junipers, and apples. The house was by now shaded from both summer sun and winter storms. Savage's wheat field had filled with new dwellings, and Denver had washed over our rural setting. The Highline Canal remained, and a coil of rope still hung down from a cottonwood branch on which we had swung out over the water nearly fifty years earlier. Erik, Frank, and I and our families gathered in the living room where Don had once sat on the floor holding Christmas chickens. Nearly all our children were there along with an especially close elderly couple my parents had known for years. We all said Don would not have wanted a large fuss. The nine grandchildren with new spouses and one great-grandchild all squeezed into the little living room by the fireplace. The grandchildren had all known Don in his big chair in the years since he retired. From that chair, he had done for them what earlier he had done for us talking at night from the end of the bed. Only one of my children could not come to the gathering because he was far overseas and simply unable to get a ticket home, and for that bad fortune he may have suffered the most of any of us.

We had trouble speaking. Throats were too full. Tears were everywhere. My mother kept her composure. She was as heroic then as during the war years and talked us all through the remembering. Then she asked—and this was the only request that she made for herself—that I would "write something" someday.

"Someday," I said.

Our century of wars had produced not only pain but also a man of ultimate decency and civility, of unbending integrity and fairness. It wouldn't be fair, he often said, to see only the evil part of this century, to see the degeneration without also seeing how much money middle-class Americans give to charity, and how poor people can get a public education for the first time in history. Or how our children are no longer working in the mines or how the law is now a step above the whims of Kaiser Wilhelm and the kings of England.

Or, he might just smile on a sunny afternoon and say, "Have you noticed how lovely your mother is today?" Just a sentence. Not very often. But often enough to make us think maybe, for such a woman, somebody ought to go weed the asparagus. He was forever fair, and if you looked at the whole picture, even a small boy could tell that doing dishes and weeding the asparagus were fair.

Don resisted the temptation to place blame outside on people of less advantage. *An objective person,* he said, *is not invested in proving what is bad. Negativity may be just a way to get your attention.* In that sense, seeing both sides, including the good, he was more a realist than many of us.

In 1953 my father wrote to the principal of the school that I attended in Switzerland and included his last prescription for my preparation for the world as he saw it:

*With respect to classes, we should like
Craig to have both chemistry and physics. If
we add to this trigonometry, French, and German, he shall be fairly busy. We are particularly desirous that he develop some proficiency
in French. To what extent it may be possible
for him to take additional work we must leave
to your judgment. If there is opportunity, additional English composition and literature, and
additional history, World history or other,
would be desirable. Perhaps German should
be limited to an accelerated practical course in
order to make room for history or English? . . .
If there is remaining time, both carpentry (or
other shop work) and typing would be very
useful.*

*Speaking, debating, dramatics would be
of considerable value to Craig if he continues
according to plan.*

Idleness was way down on his list.

His plan, I think, was that I become a lawyer. And
so, eventually, I did that. I went on to practice law for
many years in Denver. I had a wonderful experience
in Colorado politics, my one real attempt to become
something like a king, running for Congress as part of
the antiwar movement in 1970. I also tried, with others,
the Denver school integration lawsuit and, again with
others, authored concepts in Colorado politics like the
Sunshine and Sunset Laws. Eventually, however, the
Arapahoe County training to control the ego overrode

the political urge and I retired from all that in part because I could hear his voice of concern about getting carried away.

My father loved language and sent me to Switzerland in part to learn German. He was pleased that during the height of the Cold War I was working in Moscow, negotiating a book in the Soviet Academy of Sciences on the process of change, and later touring Germany lecturing in German. In the 1990s he would also have been proud that I was negotiating for peace between Armenia and Azerbaijan and conducting water negotiations in Central Asia, sometimes in Russian. But the boy who stood at the corral fence and gazed at magpies drifting on the wind above the cottonwoods was still waiting to write. One hopes Don would approve, now, after all these years of outward attention, to a final looking inward toward those things that are fine. It was the lesson of the ball bearings. *You have to look for quality wherever you can,* he said, and perhaps that allows now for a written recollection of the extraordinary decency, humor, and attention to civility that my parents added to the human condition.

There is something worth remembering of the luminous, ordinary lives of people who started out on water soup, home-schooled, who carried the frontier in their bones, even on their farthest journeys, and who knew from the soil and the wind and the rising of life in the spring that almost everyone has a chance to come through the thrashing more or less golden.